DATING THE PAST
in north-eastern Wales

Dating the Past
in north-eastern Wales

Derek Williams

ISBN: 0-86381-877-3

Cover design: Sian Parri

First published in 2004 by
Gwasg Carreg Gwalch, 12 Iard yr Orsaf, Llanrwst, Wales LL26 0EH
Tel: 01492 642031   Fax: 01492 641502
e-mail: books@carreg-gwalch.co.uk   Website: www.carreg-gwalch.co.uk

About the author:
Derek Williams, Head of Geography Bala Grammar School, Hawarden Grammar School and later, Saltney High School, B.A. (Hons) Aberystwyth, M.Ed. (Geology) Bangor; Lecturer in Bangor University (Extra Mural Dept.) 1960-1997. Author of *A Quest for Snowdonia* (2001).

For Cerys, Julian and Catherine
and Abbie

Contents

PREFACE

One of the main pleasures in writing this book was the welcome which I received from generous people to their houses, farms and historic sites. Much of the information has been gathered from visits where I have seen garderobes – lavatories projecting from an external wall – of which three domestic examples are claimed for north-eastern Wales. I have examined cruck beams in houses and barns from ground level to attics. In one farmhouse I was shown a Roman silver coin – one of a large hoard found just outside the house – with the distinctive hair-style of the Emperor's wife, her name (Julia Domna) and the title 'Augusta'. In another house bright sunshine reflected the letters 'R.V.L.A.' – the mint mark for Rhuddlan – on a silver penny with the head of HENRICUS REX (Henry II). A visit to a motte and bailey castle was overshadowed by the farmer's concern with the spread of dense gorse bushes in the castle ditch, which was reducing sheep pasture. A reminder from Ron Lloyd, a retired blacksmith, showed me the punishment for misbehaviour in school in the 1950's – copying out the list of battles in the Peninsular War from a soldier's gravestone in Llanfor churchyard. For the history of the 'ghost village' of Arennig, I had to rely on the memory of someone who lived there in the 1920's and 1930's. Until I saw the splendid panorama of the Clwydian Range on a fine autumn day, I had puzzled over John Speed's reference in 1611 to Denbigh as the 'most beautiful place in northern Wales'. In the early morning sunlight at Valle Crucis Abbey the rib-vaulted Chapter House looked ready for the Abbot to read out a Chapter from the Cistercian Order to the monks awaiting their daily tasks. On the lonely Migneint moors the small bridge Pont Rhyd-y-Porthmyn (Drovers' Bridge) showed the care taken to record it in the 1690's by the vicar of Llanycil. In the red sandstone quarry at Hirwaen the poignant 'ERW - 1850' inscribed by a stonemason recorded its last day of working. In the churches, the power of the Roman Catholic Church is recalled by the sanctuary ring (in Caerwys) and the wooden horse in Llandderfel. My most memorable visit was to see James Barfoot's fine excavation of a Turnpike Trust road near Machynlleth. In an

*Hirwaen Quarry – E.R.W. 1850 inscribed by a stonemason
on the final working face of the quarry.*

excavated section he uncovered remains of horseshoes, coach-wheel flat nails and Buckley pottery. In a hillside section in solid rock where the coaches had to brake, the wheel ruts were deeply cut into the road surface.

However, not everything could be accomplished in the field and regular visits to Flintshire County Library were needed. Documents gave a contemporary account of Richard II's fateful ambush at Penmaenrhos. The *Brut y Tywysogion* (Chronicle of the Princes) gave a clear account of Henry II's fateful expedition which was halted by gale-force winds ('a tempest') and thunderstorms in the inhospitable Berwyn Mountains in August, 1165. My favourite visit to a Museum was to Ludlow where an oak beam taken from the 13th Century house in Much Wenlock was traced, by its tree rings, to the first year of its growth in AD 886.

1. A PERFECT 'FIND'
CAER GAI ROMAN FORT

The most striking evidence of Roman occupation is a wall or building surviving above ground level and made of neat, squared blocks with some lime-mortar, bricks and tiles. In northern Wales there was plenty of local stone and, even slate, but they also brought in red sandstone from their Cheshire quarries as well and bricks and tiles from their 'factory' at Holt. They often placed bits of broken tile and pottery in their walls and these can still be seen as a conspicuous infilling. They can be readily identified – about one inch thick, orange in colour, handmade and, frequently, scored – using a bowie knife blade – into diagonal lines crudely incised into the soft clay before firing. These tiles were used on the sides of a wall of a hypocaust system (hot air heating) and were scored to allow the plaster to adhere to the inside wall. Made in Holt at the XXth Legion's Tilery they were made until AD 200 and distributed to all forts in northern Wales.

At the time when Hadrian's Wall was built (AD 120) the Romans began building stone walls around their forts in northern

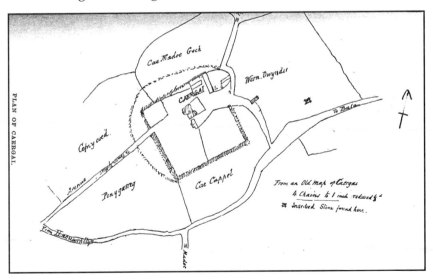

Caer Gai – an old map

Wales to replace the older earth banks and timber palisades. The best survival is the remarkable 'Hen Waliau' (Old Walls) in Caernarfon built in the early 3rd Century AD as part of a walled compound near Afon Seiont. The ruins survive to a considerable height – at least twenty courses – and are a strong reminder of Caernarfon's importance as a major fort (Segontium) and supply base.

Though not as high as Hen Waliau the Roman wall around their auxilliary fort at Caer Gai near the western end of Bala Lake is a remarkable feature which was breached in only one place to give access to the 17th Century manor house in the centre of the fort. Apart from some minor landslips the wall is intact and looks fresh especially the south face. Here the stones are clear of lichen and moss so that the geology is evident. There was no need to quarry because abundant stone – quartz, rhyolitic ash and mudstone – had been left behind by glaciers from Arennig and river deposits along the sides of the Llafar and Lliw valleys. Each of its four sides is 140 yards long but each corner is rounded to give the tell-tale 'playing-card' shape which identifies a Roman fort. In places it has twelve courses with sometimes a large orange tile left horizontally near the top almost as a gesture – 'the wall is finished'! Within Caer Gai's four acre site no Roman buildings appear at the surface and it was used as a source of ready-made stone for local churches at Llanycil, Llangywair and Llanuwchllyn according to Edward Lhuyd writing in 1698. It was recognized as a Roman fort in 1600 and 'was built at the time of the Romans as many suppose by the ancient coin of Domitian found here of late 'according to the antiquary Robert Vaughan (1592-1666). It is likely that the fort as an earth and timber construction was built in the reign of Emperor Domitian (AD 81-96); other Domitian coin finds in small forts in northern Wales indicate a period of military activity.

A field outside the south wall called 'Cae Capel' (Chapel Field) attracted attention even in 1698 when Edward Lhuyd referred to

'Kae'r Capela – where there is a pavement when the field is dry'.

In 1885 the outline of a building fifteen square feet in the centre of the field was observed in dry weather 'when the grass became scorched'. These 'parch-marks' show up in drought when grass above underground stone foundations dies off quicker than grass rooted in deeper soil which retains moisture. The parched grass shows up the outline of the buildings and can best be seen in aerial photographs. These photographs show one building which has four small rooms with two semi-circular end-rooms which may indicate a bath house. Nothing is visible at ground level but this was the normal position of a bath house on the slope just outside the walls of the fort.

Another field – 'Cae Dwyndir' (Field of rough hummocks) to the east of the fort was the scene of a find of a large red sandstone block during ploughing. The field was later called 'Cae Dentir' which refers to the tenters or frames for stretching animal skins for drying or curing. In 1885 a plough-share struck a large free-standing stone sculptured and inscribed at the base. It was part of a shrine and with evidence of urns with ashes indicated a cemetery on the road to Chester. Stones with inscribed letters are rare in northern Wales and, are usually Roman milestones. The letters are two inches deep and record the name and details of a soldier who was stationed at Caer Gai in its early days.

JULIUS SON OF GAVERONIS
A SOLDIER OF THE COHORT OF
THE NERVIANS MADE IT.

Inscribed Stone – Cae Dentir – from the Roman 'Camp' at Caergai, near Bala.

The Nervians were an auxilliary unit of the Roman army from Belgium (then part of Gaul) who were known to be in Britain in AD 105. A cohort was a unit of 480 men and this may have been the number of men stationed at Caer Gai. In the same field pottery including fine tableware or Samian pottery was found. Some of the bowls were decorated and from the patterns – flowers, animals and human figures – their source of manufacture in central France dating to AD 125-150 has been firmly established.

There is enough evidence that there was military activity from AD 90 to 150 but shortly afterwards it was abandoned, and acquired its later name 'Caer Gai'; the absence of medieval settlement was fortunate – it did not become the site of a church as happened at Caerhun or a farm. It retained its main features – the outline of the fort and the enclosing walls. Nothing has been found within the fort itself but enough is known to satisfy our curiosity about one of the finest small forts in Roman Wales.

The Romans chose it for strategic purposes but it is placed in one of the most beautiful parts of northern Wales. Westwards the Aran and Arennig mountain ranges enclose the headwaters of the Dee and its tributaries. A low pass at Pant Gwyn carries the Roman road to the fortlet at Brithdir and on to the coastal fort at Pennal. Northwards the road leads to the Roman fort at Tomen y Mur.

Caer Gai – South Wall.

2. THE HAMLET OF THE BURNING FURNACES
PENTRE FFWRNDAN AND PENTRE FARM

In the aptly-named 'Ship Field' near Flint, a small stream flowing from Halkyn Mountain entered the Dee estuary near Pentre Rock which created a small, sheltered tidal creek. Here, the harbour was deep enough – in Roman times – before the silting of the estuary for ships to proceed upriver to Chester where the Romans by the mid-50's AD had established their base and overrun the native Decangli tribes of north-eastern Wales. By AD 60, they had taken over the lead-mining areas of Halkyn Mountain and Meliden near Prestatyn. A lead ingot found at Carmel records the name C. NIPIUS ASCANIUS, who was probably a businessman who had the right to work the mines before the Roman imperial authority took over the mining rights. Lead mining had first been developed in the Mendips, with some mines opened as early as AD 49 – only six years after they had landed in Kent. In the reign of Vespasian, the Romans had begun mining in Flintshire to supply lead sheathing for water tanks and lead pipes for their new Legionary Fort at Chester (Deva) by AD 75. Three lead ingots found in Chester are inscribed to Emperor Vespasian and give an exact date of AD 74, suggesting the stockpiling of materials for building the fort.

From 1840, ploughing of Ship Field at Pentre Ffwrndan had exposed lead waste, ore (*galena*), melted lead fragments, sandstone saturated with melted lead and clearly indicated the site of lead smelting. Excavations in 1921 confirmed that on the edge of the field the Romans had built thirteen small furnaces. Each furnace consisted of a layer of gritstone flags, which formed the floor of the smelter with grey furnace waste above. The most critical evidence was provided by fragments of limestone with galena still intact and ready for smelting. The lead veins, limestone and chert sandstone were exactly the same as the country-rock at Halkyn Mountain, a short distance to the West. In Roman times it is certain that the lead veins were exposed at the surface and could be easily worked from surface deposits. In some parts of these limestone hills, veins of

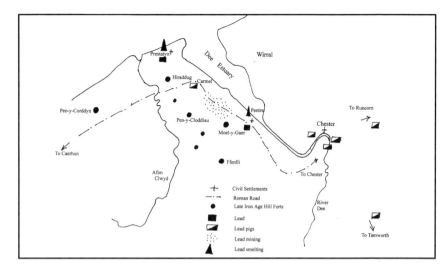

Roman Flintshire.

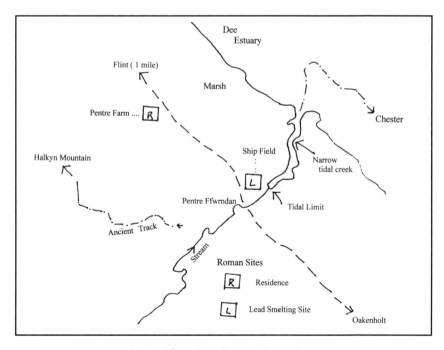

Pentre Ffwrndan – Roman Excavations.

Lead Pig – 23½" x 5½" & 4½" thick, weighing 192lbs. Found in 1886 in Roodee,
Chester, 50 yards from river Dee and 20 feet below surface.
Found with Roman pottery and coins of Vespasian and Titus.
IMP.VESP.AVG.V.T.IMP.III.S. Cast during reign of Emperor Vespasian.
Date is A.D. 74. From – DECANGL tribe (Flintshire).
(Copyright: Grosvenor Museum, Chester)

LEG XX
Part of Roman tile – 20th Legion
based at Chester (Deva).

lead can still be seen outcropping at the surface and which are still unworked. Further proof of smelting were lumps of slag, and especially fragments of lead, which were rough-ends left in the channels through which the molten lead flowed into the moulds which produced the ingots or pigs. Charcoal and even two pieces of coal were found and added further forensic archaeological evidence for smelting. The main end-products were ingots, which were 99.95% pure lead and about 170-190 lbs in weight. Apart from the ingot found at Carmel, none have been found in Flintshire though six ingots produced at 'the hamlet of the burning furnaces' (Pentre Ffwrndan) have been found in Cheshire and Staffordshire.

North-eastern Wales had, before the Romans, been in the hands of an Iron Age tribe – the Decangli – who were a sub-tribe of the Ordovices, their territory extending from Anglesey to the Severn valley. The Decangli are mentioned by name ('Decangos') by the Latin historian of the day – Tacitus – and it is thought that their land stretched from the Conwy estuary to the Dee estuary with their core being the Clwydian Range and modern-day Flintshire.

They are also known from the inscription 'DECANGL' stamped on the sides of the ingots to show that they had been produced in their territory. They lived in hill-forts on the Clwydian Range with their 'capital' at Moel Hiraddug overlooking Dyserth. They also had a major hill-fort at Moel-y-Gaer near the lead-mining area of Halkyn Mountain. One of these ingots was found in 1950 at Carmel when a foundation trench for a new village school was being dug. It was found at two feet below the surface, which suggests that it was in situ, but whether hidden deliberately or lost in transit cannot be determined. It is two feet long, 5½ inches wide and 3¾ inches deep; its find-spot is only a short distance from the main Roman road – Iter X1 – from Chester to Caernarfon (Segontium). It could have been lost in transit from Chester to one of the forts further west – Canovium, Bryn-y-Gefeiliau or Segontium – where lead products have been found. A clear moulded stamp records the name C.NIPI.ASCANI, who was a businessman who may have had the mining rights on Halkyn Mountain. The Carmel pig could be as early as AD 60 and shortly afterwards the imperial control of the mines was established and possibly they used Decangli slave labour to work them. From this time onwards, the Emperor's name and the exact dates are recorded on the ingots and the name of the tribe, such as DECANGLI (for Flintshire) and BRIG for Brigantes who lived in the northern Pennines.

Apart from the Carmel pig, three ingots were found in Chester dated AD 74-76, from their cast inscriptions, to the reign of the Emperor Vespasian. Most ingots, of course, would have been melted down to produce sheets, pipes and rings, so it is not surprising that not many have survived. Even so, two separate ingots were found in the Mersey near Runcorn and two near Tamworth. They indicate trading from Pentre Ffwrndan through the port of Chester and, perhaps, up the Mersey estuary. One of the Chester pigs was found in 1886 on the Roodee Racecourse, which was then the site of a deep-water harbour. Oak timbers were found here encased in iron tubes, which were the piles for a pier jutting out into the Dee; apart from the pig, coins, pottery and coal were found, to confirm its importance as a port.

Ship Field was, therefore, a busy lead-smelting place on the riverbank in the late 1st century and early Second Century. It produced lead ingots, and perhaps the inscribed water main found in Chester with Emperor Vespasian's name inscribed with the exact date – AD 79 – of his reign. In the 1924 excavation, debris at Ship Field included strips and sheets of lead as well as a lead ring and disc. It was also a place where people lived and left behind large quantities of pottery, including Samian ware imported from southern France (Gaul). When digging, the gleaming Samian ware catches the eye, although after nearly two thousand years in the soil its condition can change to chocolate brown. This good quality, high-gloss tableware suggests a good standard of living and most of the bowls and dishes have been traced to pottery works at Lezoux in southern Gaul. Samian pottery, with the elaborate decorations using animals, fruit, leaves and horse-shoe designs, can be used for dating. A lot of cooking pots and coarse pottery were also found, but are of no practical use for dating purposes. These finds indicate a Roman-occupied site rather than a native settlement, but there is no evidence of military control.

However, an official residence with a military character and associated with the lead smelting was found a quarter of a mile up the road – towards Flint – at the roadside Pentre Farm in 1976-7. At its finest development, the building was of stone construction with a suite of rooms, a central courtyard, an ornamental pond and a bakehouse. Two burials were uncovered with, in one case, a lead sheet and nails, which probably sealed the coffin. The building had a typical Roman bath-house with a plunge-pool and underfloor central heating (hypocaust). The military character of the building is shown by the seven tiles stamped with the XX Legion logo made for the Twentieth Legion at Chester. These were produced in the military pottery and tile works at Holt, upstream from Chester. Painted wall plaster was similar to that found at Chester, and the excavation finds indicated the house of a high-ranking official, responsible for the policing and management of the lead smelting industry at Pentre Ffwrndan in the 1st and 2nd Century AD.

3. FROM LEPTIS MAGNA TO LLANARMON
A ROMAN COIN HOARD AT LLANARMON

Thomas Griffiths, a farmer living near Llanarmon, struck lucky in March 1918, when making a drain for a small surface stream before essential ploughing in the last months of the Great War. The farmer's pick struck a hoard of Roman coins mixed with soil about two feet below the stream bed. The find spot is on the slopes of the Ceiriog valley, just north of Llanarmon, and is clearly visible from the summit of Cerrig Gwynion. This is a defended settlement or fort belonging to a pre-Roman Iron Age Tribe (c.BC500-100) situated at the top of a 1500-foot hill called Mynydd Mawr. It consists of a single wall of earth and stone with an outside ditch giving it a formidable 12-15 foot defensive system. Large outcrops of quartzite – white quartz – give it the name 'Cerrig Gwynion' (white rocks). The coin hoard was found in one place, so it may originally have been placed in a pottery jug, a leather bag or a copper box or container, and was never retrieved by the owner.

Cerrig Gwynion Iron-Age Camp near Llanarmon Dyffryn Ceiriog – Outer ditch.

18

Over the centuries, the hoard may have moved naturally down the slope from a track a short distance above and when the stream bed shifted. It is a strange place to have buried the coins with the possibility that – with the absence of Roman settlement and roads locally – someone living on Cerrig Gwynion in the early 3rd Century AD was anxious to hide this fine collection. No excavation has been carried out at Cerrig Gwynion, but eight circular hut platforms – about nine metres in diameter – can be seen clearly from aerial photographs taken in conditions of low winter sunlight.

The coins were all silver *denarii*, which was the basic unit of currency paid as wages to the Roman soldiers; some dated to BC 32, long before the Roman occupation of Britain. These early coins kept their value because they were worth their weight in silver and before deflation and debasement reduced their value. By AD 250, the silver content had fallen to only 50% fine silver. Under Emperor Septimius Severus, the rate of pay had increased to 450 denarii a year, and by the time of the burial of the coins the soldiers were receiving 675 denarii a year. Deductions for food and equipment were paid for out of this allowance. Large quantities of coinage were needed and increased during periods of military activity, such as the reign of Severus, who came over to Britain on a major campaign.

The coins at Llanarmon were found together and were originally in a container, which later perished, so that they became encrusted with soil and, according to the farmer in 1918, some 'were left behind in the drain'. In all, 551 coins were found, and of those sent to the British Museum for identification, thirty were kept at the Museum to fill gaps in their collection. The coins were generally in fine condition and most of them were read and identified from their portraits and legends. The name and portrait of the Emperor or his wife and, on the reverse side, slogans or references to virtues or the Gods, gave an exact date for each coin. Coins are the most useful artefact for the archaeologist as, for instance, when a coin embedded deliberately in the mortar of a wall at Segontium (Caernarfon) was 'evidence at once certain and precise that it was built within a few years of AD 350'. The most

Roman coin-hoard found in 1918
in marsh to left of sheep.

Llanarmon hoard.
Coins in the British Museum.
Top right (top row) Septimius Severus.
Left (second row) Julia Domna.
(by courtesy of the British Museum)

interesting feature of the Llanarmon hoard is the great number of coins falling within the reign of Emperor Septimius Severus; there are about 300 in all, if coins of his wife, Julia Domna, and other family members are included. This period of time included the well-documented imperial expedition to Britain under the personal command of Severus in AD 270, which brought 50,000 soldiers to Britain in an attempt to regain northern England after serious incursions by the Scots. Payment in wages to these extra soldiers would have brought vast quantities of coins into circulation. Severus took the title 'BRITANNICUS', and coins were issued to commemorate the success of his campaign.

Septimius Severus was called the 'African Emperor', but he was descended from Roman settlers in what is now called Libya. He was born in AD 145, and brought up in the coastal city of Leptis Magna. Later, when he became Emperor, he extensively rebuilt

Leptis Magna, giving it a theatre, market, Forum with Law Courts and fine mosaics showing gladiators in contest. He became a Senator in Rome after leaving Leptis and then became a military commander in Syria. On the death of his wife, he married Julia Domna, a beautiful and cultured woman, whom he had met previously in Syria. She spoke Latin, Greek and Aramaic, and was noted for her sense of fashion and exotic hairstyle. She appears with Severus on sculptures in Rome and there is a life-like portrait of them painted on a wooden plaque, which was found, perfectly preserved, in 1936 in Egypt. They are so well known from these sources that even the non-expert can readily identify them from their portraits on coins issued at this time. Julia Domna accompanied Severus on his military expeditions and medallions and coins show her active participation in imperial affairs. The Emperor honoured his wife with the new prestigious title 'Augusta', which is shown on the coins. Julia accompanied Severus on his fateful AD 207 expedition to Britain; he was then over sixty years old and in poor health. Although coins show him riding to war, he was suffering from gout and arthritis and was carried on a litter. After a successful campaign in Scotland, during which many forts were built, he returned south and died in York in AD 211. Coins with his wife's portrait had been issued during the reign and continued until AD 217. The large number of coins found at Llanarmon are probably linked with Severus' campaign, when vast quantities of money flooded into Britain. That the coins were used in trade with the local Celtic tribes, or that the Roman had temporarily occupied Cerrig Gwynion, are possible theories to explain how the coins found their way to Llanarmon.

Evidence of this military activity is provided by two superb relics in northern Wales, which date to Severus' reign. Unknown to the mysterious person who had buried the coins at Llanarmon at this time, the Headquarters at the big fort of Segontium (Caernarfon) was undergoing a major refit. The Romans rebuilt the aqueduct conveying water to the fort which is recorded on a slate plaque in the Museum of Segontium. A milestone to Septimius Severus – now in Bangor University Museum – was placed on the main road (Iter XI) from Segontium to Chester. They were also building a secret underground strong-room at the HQ at Segontium as a vault for denarii and the battle standards. Steps leading to this cellar are still intact and the cement floor sealed nine denarii, including coins of Severus and Julia Domna. The latest coin gives a date of AD 222, only four years earlier than the hoard at Llanarmon. These nine coins are only a small sample of the vast number of coins then being handled at Segontium.

In recent years, a few more denarii have been found near the 1918 find-spot at Llanarmon, and it was easy to identify a coin of Julia Domna with the curled hairstyle and legend 'Augusta' on the coin. On the reverse side there was a figure of one of the virtues – Hilaritas – holding a palm tree. The coin had a greenish tinge before cleaning, which probably came from the high copper content of the coin itself. By the end of the 2nd century AD, the silver content of the denarius had been reduced several times, and by the time of Julia Domna was only 50% fine silver. The latest dated coin at Llanarmon is of the year AD 226, and because of its fine unworn condition, it can be assumed that the hoard was secretly buried soon after that date.

The AD 220's have produced several hoards, including the largest hoard of 9,261 denarii found recently (1998) at Shapwick near Glastonbury. It was found by metal detector under the floor of a previously unknown villa belonging to a person of great wealth. Uncannily, the coins have almost exactly the same dates as those at Llanarmon, and the last coin is dated AD 224 and soon afterwards the hoard was buried. The Llanarmon hoard may, therefore, reflect a wider pattern of a period of anxiety, uncertainty and insecurity after the strong military regime of Septimius Severns.

4. AS STEEP AS EARTH AND RUBBISH CAN STAND
TOMEN-Y-RHODWYDD

'Castell' (castle) is an unexpected place-name for a small farmhouse situated near Llandegla. The name is mentioned as early as 1509 and refers to the medieval castle of Tomen-y-Rhodwydd, which stands in a field near the farm. It seems a strange place to site a castle, but in the Middle Ages it was well-placed to control a number of routes at the northern 'frontier' of the Kingdom of Powys. It is situated at the eastern end of the narrow, winding pass of Nant-y-Garth before its steep descent into the Vale of Clwyd. Even today, with its 30-odd bends in the road, the pass is still formidable. In the Middle Ages, with its torrential streams and steep, forested slopes, it would have been the perfect site for an ambush.

The origin of the castle is well documented in the reliable *Brut y Tywysogion* (Chronicle of the Princes) as being built in 1149 by Owain Gwynedd, who was then actively pursuing a policy of expansion of Gwynedd from his main base in Snowdonia. He was taking advantage of the civil war in England, when King Stephen was distracted during the anarchy of 'The Nineteen Long Winters'. During this period, when torture, fighting and cruelty were endemic, it was stated that 'Christ and his disciples slept'. This allowed Owain, Prince of Gwynedd, to expand southwards and eastwards into north-eastern Wales. He annexed Mold and Ystrad Alyn in 1146, Tegeingl (now, Flintshire) as far as the walls of Chester in 1149 and, also in the same year, took control of the important commote (district) of Iâl around Llandegla, which had previously belonged to Powys.

The construction of Tomen-y-Rhodwydd in 1149 was part of this policy and, like contemporary castles in Wales, it was made of earth and stones. Although built by the Welsh, it was similar in plan and construction to the motte and bailey castles introduced nearly a hundred years earlier by the Normans and first shown in the Bayeux Tapestry. This shows five Normans, all neatly dressed in tunic and leggings, using picks and wooden shovels to dig earth and stones to build up a mound on the top of which a wooden tower was being built. The Norman soldiers are working hard under the supervision of an officer holding a pennant to show his authority. The first documented castle of this type built in northern Wales was at Cymer near Dolgellau, which was built (and destroyed) in 1116. Tomen-y-Rhodwydd is a typical motte and bailey castle with a large mound 25 feet in height, a diameter of 60 feet and with a completely flat top on which the wooden keep would have been built. This motte stands at one end of an oval enclosure – the bailey – and would have been enclosed by a high wooden fence or palisade and a gatehouse. The junction of the bank of the bailey with the motte shows that they were built at the same time and of the same local materials – limestone blocks, soil and clay. On the sides of the motte there is some evidence of a dry stone wall, but unlike a contemporary castle at Prysor, there is no evidence of the use of mortar. The garrison would have occupied the keep, with the bailey reserved for stables, stores and domestic rooms, such as the kitchen. The key to the defence would have been the motte which towers above the bailey. In 1075, when the Normans were defending their new motte and bailey castle at Rhuddlan, the Welsh, under Gruffudd ap Cynan, stormed and burnt the buildings in the bailey. Some Norman soldiers were killed, but many fled to the safety of the motte. The motte and bailey at Tomen-y-Rhodwydd was surrounded by a deep ditch and accompanying steep bank, both of which still survive. In a letter from Rev. J. Evans to Edward Llwyd in 1693, he gives a detailed description of the castle and describes 'the great ditch around the highest mount (motte) is 16-17 yards from the bottom to the top and as steep as earth and rubbish can stand'. He also mentions one entrance at the north-eastern side with some steep steps.

The building of Tomen-y-Rhodwydd was not just an indication of the growing authority of Owain Gwynedd in the power-game with Gwynedd's old rival – Powys. It was a castle deliberately planted in Iâl, which was a vital frontier district of Powys. It was a threat to the heartland of Powys Fadog in the Dee valley. The military advisers of Owain Gwynedd chose Tomen-y-Rhodwydd

Tomen-y-Rhodwydd, Llandegla.
View of the motte from the north-east near the entrance.
Deep outer ditch and outer bank now gorse covered.

Tomen-y-Rhodwydd.
(Copyright of the Clwyd-Powys Archaeological Trust CPAT 84/32/25)

for its fine position only two miles from the remarkable Horseshoe Pass, which gave easy access to the Vale of Llangollen. However, its vulnerability on the frontier was shown by the reference in *Brut y Tywysogion* to its destruction in 1157. Its short life of only eight years was ended by a raiding party under Iorwerth Goch, brother of Madog ap Maredudd, Prince of Powys, who destroyed it by fire. All the timber buildings were razed to the ground, and it was never rebuilt. The evidence left is still substantial and impressive; the entire ground plan of the castle can be seen in the field and even better from aerial photographs. The flat top of the motte (tomen) is still a suitable building site and the steep banks and deeply-cut ditches are intact; the only changes in 750 years have been due to natural soil erosion, mole hills, rabbit burrows and some damage by sheep grazing. By the 1190's, stone-built castles had appeared in northern Wales – the stone keep at Dolwyddelan may be 1190 and Gerald the Welshman (in 1188) refers in his 'Itinerary of Wales' to stone castles at Deudraeth and Garn Fadryn in Llŷn. By this time, motte and bailey castles, with their timber structures, had become redundant, but they have survived, as at Tomen-y-Rhodwydd, in remarkable condition.

Despite the large number of motte and bailey castles in Wales and the Marches – about 450 have been traced – few sites have been excavated or yielded only casual finds. Many farms along the Welsh-Shropshire border have their own castle, usually a few yards from the farmhouse itself, and a tree-covered motte now looks natural in the landscaped garden. Near Leintwardine, a farmer recently unearthed a medieval iron dagger, when he struck the bank of a motte on the edge of the lawn.

The first evidence of life in a motte and bailey castle was uncovered after twenty-five years of excavation at Hen Domen near Montgomery. It is a large castle, which was established between 1071-1093 as the impressive fortress of a Marcher Lordship. Robert of Montgomery was one of the principal barons of William the Conqueror and given the task of stabilizing the Border and extending Norman power in central Wales. The castle was excavated during twenty-five summer seasons, and apart from post-holes and timber, few archaeological finds were made. A few scraps of pottery and some nails from its early days were found. In its final days in the early 13th century, a jug (from Lincolnshire) and a coin – useful for dating purposes – were also found. An excavated pit filled with kitchen refuse – fish bones, egg shells, bones from cattle, pigs and deer – indicated a modest menu and lifestyle. An abundance of thatch and wattler-timber showed the building materials used, and with the stable-bedding for horses, were the product of local meadows, marsh and woodland similar to those in the present-day countryside. These sparse finds suggest a simple basic life led by soldiers who spent much of their time outdoors. During the 13th century, the huge castle-complex of Montgomery was built, and Hen Domen was abandoned.

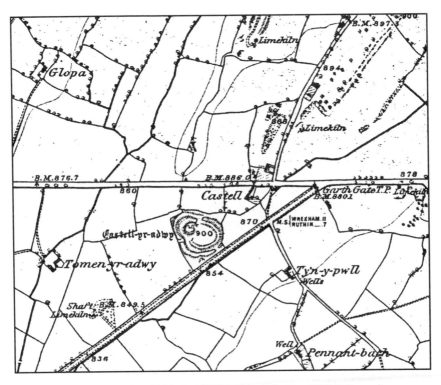

Tomen-y-Rhodwydd (shown as Castell-yr-Adwy on 1871 O.S. map)

5. A VIOLENT STORM RAGES OVER THE BERWYN MOUNTAINS
HENRY II'S INVASION OF 1165

It is not often that a small valley such as the Ceiriog – Dyffryn Ceiriog – gets a detailed mention in medieval records with references to the King – the powerful Henry II, who accompanied his army. Coming to the throne – in 1154 – of a vast Empire stretching from Scotland to the Pyrenees, he was very conscious that, despite nearly 100 years of warfare, Wales was still independent. A few years earlier (1137), a strong ruler had emerged in northern Wales – Owain Gwynedd – who had extended his authority across Flintshire and taken the mighty Norman fortress at Mold. Henry, in retaliation, brought a large army from Chester, and he was almost captured in an ambush in the woods at Ewloe, near Hawarden. Henry's army pushed across Flintshire, re-captured Rhuddlan castle. Owain was forced into a truce and gave Henry some hostages, and allowed the King to keep the land around Rhuddlan.

The truce was broken in 1165 when Henry determined to reduce Owain's position to that of an Earl owing allegiance to the King. He collected a vast army of soldiers from Anjou, Brittany, Gascony, Normandy, Flanders and men from northern England. He proceeded from Shrewsbury to the Welsh border at Oswestry with the aim of crossing the trackless wastes of the Berwyn Mountains and striking at the heart of Welsh power in Snowdonia. The story is first recorded by Gerald the Welshman only twenty three years afterwards, when it was still fresh, but he only records a battle near Oswestry, without giving the exact site. The details are fully recorded in *Brut y Tywysogion* – The Chronicle of the Princes – written later. It says that the King brought his army to Oswestry, and that the Welsh had based their army in the Vale of Edeyrnion at Corwen, so the two armies were separated by the Berwyn Mountains. Owain Gwynedd also had the military support of Lord Rhys of Deheubarth (south-western Wales) and the local war-lord, Prince of Powys, which was a rare alliance. During the long days

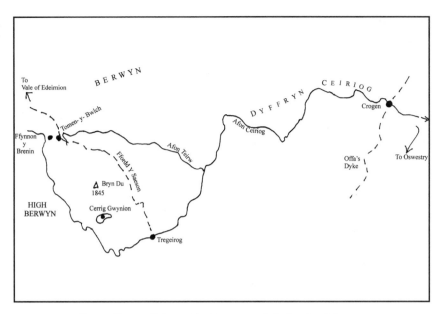

Henry II's expedition to the Berwyn and the Battle of Crogen.

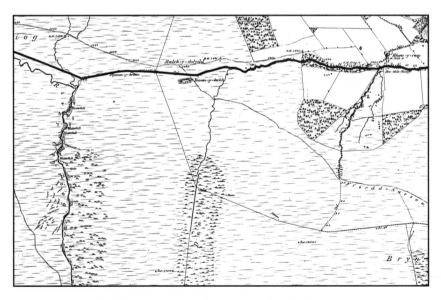

Ffordd y Saeson running north westwards towards
Tomen y Bwlch and Ffynnon y Brenin.

Battle of Crogen.
Floodplain of river Ceiriog near Castle Mill and near Offa's Dyke (right).

of the summer of 1165, there was no engagement, but Owain was aware of Henry's intentions from intelligence conveyed through beacon fires from Oswestry to Tomen y Gwyddel in Dyffryn Ceiriog and the Berwyn summits. Henry, growing impatient, moved his army northwards from Oswestry to the Ceiriog valley at Chirk, which was the main routeway through the Berwyn to Owain's army at Corwen. Dyffryn Ceiriog was almost impenetrable due to the dense oak forests, so Henry ordered large numbers of tree-fellers to cut down and clear the forested valley bottom. It was at this time that a skirmish took place that has been called the 'Battle of Crogen'. A party of Welsh soldiers had broken away from the army at Corwen, who 'in the absence of their leaders', chose the narrowest part of the valley where the Offa's Dyke crossed the valley floor. It was precisely in this narrow gap that the bloody encounter took place, with many killed on both sides. It is traditionally held that the soldiers were buried in the bank of Offa's Dyke at the sides of the valley and this gap is still

Cerrig Gwynion.
Summit of white quartz rocks. Earthworks on left is later
– could have been site of Henry II's camp in Monte Berwyn.

known as 'Adwy'r Beddau' – the 'Gap of the Graves'. On the modern map, this site is shown as Castle Mill and the 'battlefield' is the floodplain on either side of the bridge. In medieval times, the area was known as 'Crogen', hence the skirmish is known as the 'Battle of Crogen'. The place-name 'Crogen' still survives in the names of farms within half a mile of the battle site – Crogen Wladys, Crogen Iddon Isaf and Crogen Iddon Uchaf. Fighting was ferocious and the word 'Crogen' got into the military vocabulary of the English army as 'courage'. King Henry was almost killed in the fighting and was protected by the shield of Hubert de Clare, Constable of Colchester castle.

Henry was now anxious to engage the Welsh army, who were still in their tents at Corwen, so he moved up Dyffryn Ceiriog and 'pitched his tents in the Berwyn mountains'. It is likely that he followed the Ceiriog up to Tregeiriog and then turned up a side valley on to the moors. The site of the King's camp has not been identified, but he would have needed a large level-topped area

31

with some defensive features. The most likely possibility is the Iron Age camp at Cerrig Gwynion, which even today retains strong ramparts and ditches. It also had direct access to the easiest crossing of the Berwyn to the Vale of Edeyrnion. Nearby, an old road – 'Ffordd y Saeson' – runs north-westwards to a gap in the Berwyn watershed. This road still exists as a track and is shown on the early O.S. maps as 'Ffordd y Saeson' or 'The road of the English'. In 1908, an old lady in Tregeiriog, where it starts, referred to it as 'Stryd Fawr' – the 'Great Street'. It may, therefore, be part of the oral tradition of the memory of Henry's notable expedition of 1165. It rises steeply up the valley from Tregeiriog, and is still used as a farm road today until it reaches the open moorland, where it survives as a well-defined track. It is six feet wide in places, with banks on either side, which can be followed easily as it makes its way across cotton grass, heather and occasional peat bogs. It keeps to the drier eastern slopes of Bryn Du – probably its best exposure – and strikes north-westwards passing cairns or burial mounds, some of which have been levelled. It reaches the valley at Tomen y Bwlch – another burial mound – and passes near the strangely-named 'Ffynnon y Brenin' – 'The King's Well'. In 1913, when a ruined structure still existed, it was described by the Royal Commission as 'a mountain spring in a boggy area a few yards south of the northern boundary of Llanarmon parish and a little south of Ffordd y Saeson. It probably refers to Henry II's expedition'. Parts of the road are paved in places and at one point one large slab as big as a long farm table has been laid across a boggy section. Although no evidence has been found, the road may have been built, or at least used, by Henry's army.

After setting up camp here – somewhere at or near Cerrig Gwynion – Henry 'stayed a few days. And then, there came upon them a mighty tempest of wind and bad weather and rain, and lack of food and then he moved his tents back to England' (*Brut y Tywysogion*).

Henry's army was in a good strategic position awaiting the Welsh foot soldiers expected to come from the Vale of Edeyrnion through the low gap clearly visible on the skyline. But Henry's large army was in an exposed position and at the end of an extended supply line from Shrewsbury. Food for his large army of foot soldiers and forage for the horses were severely disrupted by this exceptional 'tempest' – deluge of rain and high winds. Rather than risk a battle, Henry decided to retreat to the Borders and to find the security of Chester. The soldiers from Gascony were probably greatly relieved to dismantle their tents after this fateful thunderstorm in the Welsh mountains!

It is still necessary to keep an open mind on the details of this episode in Welsh History. Maps did not exist at this time and it is fortunate that place-names such as 'Berwyn Mountains', 'Dyffryn Ceiriog' and 'Vale of Edeyrnion' are mentioned so that it is possible to piece together a rudimentary account of the geography of the expedition. Even place-names such as 'Ffordd y Saeson' and 'Ffynnon y Brenin' and the burial mounds cannot be discounted in the search for the route of Henry's expedition.

No archaeological evidence exists to pin-point the exact site of Henry's camp in 'Monte Berwyn', but Cerrig Gwynion – the Iron Age hill-fort north of Llanarmon – is the best 'fit'. It lies only one mile from Ffordd y Saeson and it has a large level space at the summit protected by two and – in places, three, walls and ditches. Significantly, the south-east curve is breached by the dyke of a much later earthwork. This large oval enclosure is sheltered by the high quartz-rock outcrops at the summit which give Cerrig Gwynion its appropriate name 'White Rocks'. If the oval enclosure could be dated to the early Medieval period, it would strengthen the case for this marvellous site at Cerrig Gwynion as Henry's fateful camp in August 1165.

EXTRACT FROM *BRUT Y TYWYSOGION* ('CHRONICLE OF THE PRINCES') FOR THE YEAR 1165

And he returned again to England and gathered a host beyond number of the picked warriors of England and Normandy and Flanders and Gascony and Anjou and all the North and Scotland. And he came to Oswestry, thinking to annihilate all Welshmen. And against him came Owain and Cadwaladr, sons of Gruffudd ap Cynan, and all the host of Gwynedd with them, and Rhys ap

Gruffudd and with him the host of Deheubarth, and Owain Cyfeiliog and Iorwerth Goch ap Maredudd and the sons of Madog ap Maredudd and the host of all Powys with them, and the two sons of Madog ab Iorwerth and their host. And they gathered together fearlessly and boldly into Edeirnion, and pitched tents there at Corwen. And as they were thus on both sides staying in their tents, without the one daring to attack the other, at last the king of England was enraged; and he moved his host into the wood of Dyffryn Ceiriog, and he had that wood cut down, and felled to the ground. And there a few picked Welshmen, in the absence of their leaders, manfully and valorously resisted them. And many of the bravest on either side were slain. And the king and his armies advanced, and he pitched his tents on the Berwyn mountain. And he stayed there a few days. And then there came upon them a mighty tempest of wind and bad weather and rains, and lack of food; and then he moved his tents into England. And in rage he had the eyes of the hostages, who had been long kept with him, gouged out; namely, two sons of Owain's, Rhys and Cadwallon, and Cynwrig and Maredudd, sons of Rhys, and several others. And for the second time, after he had changed his counsel, he moved a host to Chester. And there he encamped many days, until ships from Dublin and from the other towns of Ireland came to him. But since that number of ships was not sufficient for him, he rewarded the ships of Dublin with much wealth and sent them back to their land. And he himself and his host returned a second time to England.

The *Brut y Tywysogion* or 'Chronicle of the Princes' is a reliable account of the main events in medieval Welsh History until the year 1282, when Wales was conquered by Edward I. Written in a monastery soon afterwards, it is thought that it was written in the Cistercian Abbey of Strata Florida in Ceredigion. By a coincidence, it was recorded in 1165 that 'a community of monks *came* to the place called Strata Florida'. Written in Latin, it sometimes records eye-witness accounts of an event; the sympathies of the Welsh-speaking monks is usually evident in the accounts. There were probably a number of copies, which became lost after the Dissolution of the Monasteries in 1536.

6. MAKING A MINT OF MONEY IN RHUDDLAN
A SHORT-CROSS PENNY FOUND IN FLINT

Finding a coin is always interesting, particularly when it is 800 years old and still in good condition. Such a coin was found about twenty-two years ago, when the owner of a new house on the western outskirts of Flint was digging his garden and thought he had turned up a shiny button. On cleaning it up, he realised that it was a silver coin almost exactly the same size as a modern penny, but much thinner. The clear engraving of a cross at the centre of the reverse side showed that it was a 'short-cross penny', with the King's name HENRICUS on the obverse side giving its period of issue rather than its exact date. The King's crown consists of nine pellets and his hairstyle is shown as small curved strokes. The medieval face with moustache and beard completes the silver-smith's representation of the all-powerful King. The name 'HENRICUS REX' is inscribed around the rim of the coin and refers to Henry II who reigned from 1154 to 1189. The reverse side has a double-lined cross with pellets in each of its angles as well as pellets at the end of each line. Around the outer rim, the name of the moneyer is inscribed as well as the name of the mint given as an abbreviation. The important information on this coin is given by the letters 'ON ON RVLA', which gives a clue to the name of the moneyer and the mint.

The silver penny had been the standard coin of England for centuries, dating back to King Offa. But by 1154, when Henry II succeeded to the throne, the coinage had been seriously debased during the civil war of Stephen and Matilda. During this wretched period of 'the Nineteen long winters when Christ and his Saints slept', coins were clipped, base silver was used, coins were low in weight and in the absence of a strong central authority, the warring barons issued their own coins, even using their own portraits. As befitted a King ruling a major empire stretching from Scotland to the Pyrenees, Henry II restored order to the currency and in 1180 introduced the 'short-cross penny' as the standard coin of the

Short-cross Penny of Henry II found in Flint.

realm. It has a portrait with a crown of pellets and the names 'HENRICUS REX' were stamped imperiously on the head side of the newly minted coins. Henry died in 1189 so that it might be thought that the coin found at Flint could be clearly dated to 1180-1189, but that is not the case. The short-cross penny continued to be issued with the inscription 'HENRICUS REX' during the succeeding reigns of Richard I (1189-99), John (1199-1216) and even into the reign of Henry III until 1247. During this long time-span, Henry's name was retained and the short-cross design continued substantially as it was in 1180. There are, however, some clues to indicate whether the coins were issued during the reign of Richard or John. The King's face is thinner; hair is shown as short curved strokes, nine pellets are used instead of eight in Henry's coins. Another major clue for dating is the name of the moneyer, as will be shown later.

It has been known from the early 20th Century that a coin with the letters 'RVLA' indicates that the coin was minted in Rhuddlan. Part of the inscription is missing so that 'ON ON RVLA' reads

Short-cross Penny of Henry II found in Flint.
RVLA . . . Rhuddlan Mint.

'SIMON AT RHUDDLAN', which is the standard practice used at this time for denoting the name of the moneyer and his mint. Pipe Roll manuscripts give the names of four moneyers at Rhuddlan during this period, and they fortunately correspond broadly with the reigns of the four Kings involved in short-cross issues. Halli's name appears in the time of Henry II followed by Tomas in Richard I's reign and Simon during King John's reign. These consecutive moneyers struck coins intermittently until 1214, when production ceased and was resumed by moneyer Henricus in 1240-47.

The coins from Rhuddlan were of good weight, but the dies used were of rougher workmanship than those used at the main mints at London (LVND) and Canterbury (CANTE). Rhuddlan coins have been found in Newry (Ireland), Lisieux (France), Colchester and Eccles in Cheshire so it would be expected that some would also be found in Flintshire. Apart from the Flint coin, an identical coin was found by using a metal-detector one and a half miles away on a steep, wooded slope. This was a casual find, but was found near the earth and timber castle on Hen Blas built by Henry II in 1157. In excavations at Hen Blas, a broken, corroded coin of King John was found and dated to 1210; seven other similar coins were found nearby in a layer of charcoal. Such a large number of short-cross pennies of the same period suggest a lot of activity.

Each coin found with the all-important mintmark 'RVLA' adds to our knowledge of Rhuddlan's importance, which is mentioned as having a mint ('moneta') in Domesday Book (1086). Rhuddlan ('Rolent' in Domesday Book) was held by Robert for Earl Hugh of Chester as a distant frontier post against the Welsh. Its importance is shown by the fact that it had a castle – now a grassy mound overlooking the river Clwyd – a church, a mill, a mint and the eighteen burgesses denoted its status as a town. Some coins of William Rufus (1090) have been found in excavations locally, but no evidence of the actual mint has survived; it is only rarely that archaeological evidence of a medieval mint survives even in such large towns as London. A few dies have been found in excavations in London. The mint would have been a workshop, where sheets of silver would have been brought in and the moneyer would oversee the cutting of the valuable metal and the hammering of the dies for producing the individual coin by hand. The coins would then be scrupulously weighted and the moneyer's name and mint would guarantee the legality of the issue.

The coin found at Flint had been minted at Rhuddlan at some date between 1199 and 1205 in the first half of the reign of King John when he was on good terms with his son-in-law, Llywelyn the Great, who had married John's daughter, Joan. From its good condition, it was probably lost soon after it had been minted and most probably in the second half of John's reign, when his relations with Llywelyn deteriorated. The find-spot is only 12 miles from Rhuddlan and may have been lost, like others at Hen Blas, by a soldier in the pay of the Earl of Chester. The area west of Flint was on the military route from Chester to the outpost at Rhuddlan. At the beginning of John's reign, the Earl of Chester, Ranulf, was under siege at Rhuddlan castle and was relieved by forces under Roger de Lacey, marching from Chester.

In 1211, John himself and a large army assembled at Oswestry and marched through Flintshire as far as Rhuddlan and then on to Deganwy to assert his authority against his rebellious son-in-law, Llywelyn. The coins at Flint and Hen Blas could, therefore, have been lost in this period (1211-15) when John re-established temporary control of Flintshire. The motte and bailey castles at Hen Blas and Bryn-y-Cŵn – only 1/2 mile from the Flint coin find-spot – would have been busy and actively garrisoned with fifty or more soldiers stationed at each castle. After John's retreat, Llywelyn recaptured Rhuddlan and closed down the mint in 1214. The Flint coin was a casual loss and remained in the unploughed pasture until the new houses were built in 1981. The attribution of the mintmark 'RVLA' as Rhuddlan is now accepted by coin experts, but these Rhuddlan coins were rare in northern Wales until the discovery of twenty-four coins at Llanfaes.

The largest find of Rhuddlan-minted coins was found recently as part of a hoard of over seven hundred coins found in one field on the edge of the small village of Llanfaes, in Anglesey. This would seem, at first sight, to be the most unlikely place for such a find, but in 12th and 13th Centuries, Llanfaes was the chief commercial centre in Gwynedd. It had a harbour shipping in wine, salt and iron and also had a weekly market and fairs, presumably held in the field where the coins were found. The coins included many short-cross pennies, with twenty-four minted in Rhuddlan and some exactly similar to the one found in Flint. Many were in fine condition and their inscriptions SIMON.ON.RVLA and HENRICUS REX can be clearly read. The king's head gives only a slight notion of what these early Norman Kings actually looked like. The medieval artist was not interested in trying to make a physical portrait of the king. The coins were minted in the King's name and stamped with this head, but were only stylised versions of the king; all that was intended was to portray the king as a symbol of authority.

It is likely that in this period – apart from John's brief occupation (1211-13) – the Rhuddlan mint was in the hands of the Welsh, who produced copies of the original English coins and were using crude dies. The Rhuddlan mint may have used silver from Halkyn Mountain, which was only seven miles away. Mining here is mentioned by Gerald the Welshman in his famous 'Itinerary of Wales' made in 1188. He stated that ' . . . we proceeded from Rhuddlan to the small cathedral of St Asaph; from whence we continued our journey through a country rich in minerals of silver, where many are sought in the bowels of the earth (Halkyn Mountain), to the little cell of Basingwerk (abbey) where we spent the night'.

There is evidence from Gwynedd at this time that the Welsh Princes were in need of increasing supplies of coinage, as the bartering of goods was being replaced by the use of money at such commercial centres as Llanfaes. Later, in 1282, Edward I conquered Gwynedd and removed the entire population of the village to his new town of Newborough in the south-west corner of Anglesey. He replaced Llanfaes with the castle, borough and port of Beaumaris. The seven hundred coins found at Llanfaes are a valuable legacy of its earlier importance under the Welsh Princes.

Motte and Bailey castle at Rhuddlan (Twt Hill). River Clwyd on left.

7. A TUDOR 'MAKE-OVER'
FOR A MEDIEVAL HOUSE
LLYS EURYN, LLANDRILLO-YN-RHOS

Llandrillo-yn-Rhos church lies on a 'five-star' site perched on a hill-top overlooking the sea and limestone headlands. A tombstone of Ednyfed Fychan in the north aisle and the later south aisle built by the Ladies of Conwy, give a focus on the history of the area and especially the nearby-fortified house of Llys Euryn. Although it is now only a ruin, Llys Euryn has been expertly restored and conserved – a thorough 'face-lift' – by the work of Conwy Council, CADW and the Gwynedd Archaeological Trust. The house is open to the public and clear information notice boards help to give an understanding of its complex history.

The tombstone of Ednyfed Fychan in the church lies in the 13th Century north aisle, at a time when it was known as 'Dinerth', and Ednyfed Fychan, a local lord, was appointed in Seneschal or the Chancellor to the all-powerful Prince of northern Wales – Llywelyn-ap-Iorwerth. He gave prudent advice to Llywelyn and was a skilled negotiator with the English King, Henry III, and the Earl of Chester. Ednyfed had estates in Anglesey and in neighbouring Creuddyn and, for his services, was granted in 1230, land in Rhos Fynach in a charter given by Llywelyn. He was granted the land of Rhos Fynach – centred on Llandrillo – extending from Bryn Euryn to the sea with woods, meadows, pastures, paths and streams. For this, he had to pay an annual rent of two shillings to 'God and the Church of Dinerth towards lamps at Eastertide'. The charter gave the boundaries of the land – ditches, watercourses and banks – and is dated May 1230 with the green wax seal of Llywelyn and the print of a man in armour. The tag attached to the parchment seal was a twist of silk and the witness was David, 'our heir', who was the younger son of Llywelyn and Joan, daughter of King John, and he succeeded his father in 1240.

It has been thought that Ednyfed Fychan built a house in this newly-acquired land and that it was, at least in part, Llys Euryn on the flat limestone ledge above Llandrillo church. If built in 1230, it would have been a large communal house – a large hall with a central hearth. It would have been built of timber on rubble foundations and similar to the Llys of Llywelyn, which has been recently uncovered under the sand hills near Newborough in Anglesey. At Llys Euryn, there is strong evidence of such a rubble foundation, which contrasts sharply with the neat limestone blocks, which now form the walls. There is also a large grindstone which was re-used at the base of a doorway and probably dates to the mid or early 13th Century. There are also traces of small, squared stones laid on regular courses and using thin slates similar to other contemporary buildings in northern Wales. These small-scale pieces of evidence could indicate a 13th Century occupation and the remains of the Llys of Ednyfed Fychan. In the absence of medieval finds, this must remain only a possibility, but the stratigraphy of the ground has not been disturbed, so that future excavation may still yield evidence.

By the mid 15th Century, it is likely that the Llys had become derelict, but its site had attracted the attention of a local chieftain, Gruffudd ap Goch, who lived in the old house of Graianllyn up the valley from Mochdre. Loyalty to blood ties were then stronger than allegiance to authority, and lawless conditions prevailed over most of northern Wales. Little is known of Gruffudd ap Goch's lifestyle, but vicious feuds between rural families, with their armed retainers, were common. In Sir John Wynn's *History of the Gwydyr Family,* written only three generations later, there is a vivid account of how his great grandfather, Meredith ap Ieuan, needed twenty tall bowmen to accompany him and his family to the newly-built church (1500) at Dolwyddelan in the wilds of Nant Conwy. They were needed to prevent an ambush on their return home from church, and look-outs were also posted on the hills.

These local family disputes were also exacerbated by the Wars of the Roses, in which Conwy castle was in contention between the Yorkist and Lancastrian factions. In an incident, one of Gruffudd ap Goch's sons – Rhys – was killed and his other sons, Robin and Howell, avenged his death by storming the castle and beheading the constable. Later, Robin rebuilt or restored the house at Llys

Llys Euryn.

Euryn for his eldest son, Hugh, who adopted the English-style name 'Conway' or 'Conwy' after the river. Contemporary bards are full of praise of the new house, referring to it as a fortress with towers, three-storeys high and built of freestone. It is likely that this is the house which is substantially the one which we can see today. The family, towards the end of the 15th Century, had greatly increased its status; his son, also Hugh, had married Elizabeth, who was the daughter of the powerful Thomas Salusbury of Lleweni. This gave a family connection with Henry, Earl of Richmond, who defeated Richard III at Bosworth and became King. Hugh Conwy, in armour and with a body of retainers, was on the winning side under Henry's banner and benefited – financially and socially – after the memorable summer of 1485. He became one of the Privy Chamber of the King and was granted mining concessions.

This new house – much of which is still standing – is of the design and shows a house which was fortified using castle-style building methods. The walls were over three feet thick and the neat limestone blocks were set in strong lime mortar. The 'windows' were arrow-loops, with an aperture of only three inches on the outside wall. The only surviving doorway is a narrow, pointed arch only six feet high, thirty inches wide and easy to defend. It was closed at night by a massive timber drawbar with the wall sockets still intact. Drawbars on houses of the gentry continued in use until the 17th Century. At the four corners of the building there were garderobes (lavatories) on the outer walls and, as square shafts, were copies of those found on medieval castles. The builders were thinking of defence and even siege. All of these features indicate a medieval hall-house, with a square plan and a central hearth fireplace with an open hole or louvre in the timbered roof.

By the reign of Queen Elizabeth, the Conwy family were at the height of their wealth, and it was the home of a High Sheriff which was then a prestigious office. Great improvements were made to a house which had previously been medieval in character. A new era of house building in northern Wales had begun, with new features – more private rooms, more specialist rooms such as kitchens, fireplaces with external chimneys, large windows using the new material (glass). Inside, there were rich tapestries, carvings, plasterwork and painted walls. Decorative plaster ceilings and even initials and a coat of arms in plaster over the new fireplaces were a high status symbol.

During the 17th Century, the Conway family continued in the female lines and the 'Ladies of Conway' continued to live here with little income and, apart from disrepair, the house suffered from fire damage to the west hall. Margaret Conway died in 1654 – her gravestone can be seen in Llandrillo churchyard and she was probably the last occupant. A coin dated 1701 from the courtyard at Llys Euryn and clay pipes of this period may have been casual losses by visitors or by workmen. In its final phase, all the useful building materials – glass, slate, timber and dressed stone – were removed and some of the walls completely demolished. An estate map of c.1763 does not show any roads or tracks leading up to the house, and when Pennant visited it in 1784, he described it as 'a large ruined house'. The remaining walls, with their narrow doorway and arrow-loops, have survived almost unchanged up to the present. Even the put-logs – square holes through the walls – for timber scaffolding during construction and timber holes for floor beams have survived in this historic building.

8. THE MOST BEAUTIFUL PLACE
IN NORTHERN WALES
DENBIGH FRIARY

In the 13th Century, religious orders of friars which were founded included the Carmelite or 'White Friars', who depended on alms obtained be begging. They were unlike the Cistercian monks who preferred to live 'far from the haunts of men' and tended to establish themselves in or near towns. One such Carmelite friary was built on the meadows on the eastern outskirts of the castle-town of Denbigh. The local landowner, Sir John Salusbury, gave the land which, in 1284, was part of the Lleweni estate and they were welcomed here by the Lord of Dyffryn Clwyd, Reginald de Grey. His uncle had taken part in the Crusades and introduced the Carmelite Order – inspired by a group of religious hermits living on Mount Carmel in Palestine – to England in 1250.

In 1284, a lot of building was taking place in the area under Reginald de Grey, who was granted the castle at Ruthin to oversee these changes introduced after Edward I's conquest of Wales. The

Denbigh Friary 1742 by S. & N. Buck.

friary was being built at the same time as Denbigh castle, and both were using limestone from Graig Quarry less than a mile away. The friary was built to house the friars, so that it had a hall, kitchen, buttery and a dormitory above. As befitted a religious order, the main building was the chapel, which has remained to this day, although in a ruined condition. There are three walls rising to roof level, which indicate the imposing scale of the original building. Its existing features include two canopied seats (sedilia) set in the south wall, where the priests sat during the service. The perforated stone basin used for holding water for rinsing the chalice and plates after mass is still intact.

The Salusbury family, who lived at Lleweni, a short distance across the fields, were great benefactors and the founder, Sir John, was buried at the Friary on 2nd March 1289. Other members of the family were also buried there until 1536, when the Dissolution of the religious houses took place under Henry VIII. At the time of the Dissolution of the religious houses, the Friary was then only a small house with six friars but over the years it had grown to include outbuildings, stables, gardens and orchards. The mendicant, or begging friars, had been a familiar sight in medieval Denbigh, begging for alms for distribution to the poor and attending mass at the town church of St Marcella's. Until 1813, a nearby street still retained its medieval name – Beggar's Lane – which recalled these times. At the time the friary was disbanded, an inventory of its possessions showed that altar cloths, candlesticks and four bells were housed in the chapel. In the domestic quarters – kitchen, buttery and malthouse – they listed pots and pans, pewter dishes and tables. The friary was granted by Henry VIII to Richard Andrews and William Lisle, but was re-acquired by the Salusbury family in a grant to Sir John by Queen Elizabeth. At this time (1610), John Speed, the map-maker to the Queen, called Denbigh 'the most beautiful place in northern Wales'. He travelled the length and breadth of England and Wales and, apart from his county maps, produced seventy town plans, including one of Denbigh. It was a very accurate map showing the castle, walls and gates and a detailed street plan of the town. The friary is shown in the top right corner of the map, on the edge of

Denbigh Friary – the remains of the church – east window bricked-up.

the town. It is certain that Speed spent some time in Denbigh and the map is the result of his own careful observation. Speed's map shows the main stream in Denbigh flowing along the northern edge of the town and through the grounds of the Friary. This water supply, and its prime position on the Ruthin-St Asaph road, made it an attractive commercial proposition. In 1742, a fine engraving by the Buck Brothers shows the chapel in good condition, surrounded by trees, bushes and river meadows. The friary outbuildings were used for wood storage and a malthouse and by the end of the 19th century, it had a hay-loft and stables. These were destroyed by fire in 1898, but the chapel survived the fire and is still an imposing ruin, although without its West Door and its roof.

DOMINICAN FRIARY – RHUDDLAN

Only a few miles across the valley, near another castle – Rhuddlan – the Dominican Friars (the Black Friars) had set up their friary. Founded by St Dominic (1171-1221), the order of black-gowned friars also rejected the possession of revenues from land and houses and were itinerant preachers, who depended for their livelihood by begging for food and clothes. They were also attracted to towns with a population often neglected by ill-educated parish priests. The Dominicans were highly trained Theologians – their first friary was in Oxford – and spread the Christian message to poor and rich alike. They travelled in twos and were allowed to preach within the limits of the territory of the friary, although people were also encouraged to attend services in the friary chapel. The poor identified easily with the begging friars, but the Dominican Order also succeeded in getting land and building materials from rich benefactors. Denbigh Friary depended on the rich Salusbury family, but Rhuddlan was able to get the full support of the Welsh prince, Llywelyn ap Gruffudd. The land itself was granted by Llywelyn ap Gruffudd in 1258, when he was at the height of his powers after the conquest of the Perfeddwlad – the Four Cantrefs of north-eastern Wales. He set up the friary in fields near the motte and bailey castle at Rhuddlan, which afforded protection. Shortly afterwards, he appointed Anian – a Welshman from Dolgellau – as the first Prior.

During the occupation of Wales by Edward I in 1282, the Dominicans gained favour with the King by attending English soldiers wounded in the war.

In 1310, the friars were in favour and given a grant of 1½ acres of land to extend the friary. The lay-out would have included a church and chapter house with cloisters, dormitories and stables. It also functioned as a farm with cornfields, meadows, orchards, cattle and pigs. By 1534, the friary had declined and housed only six friars, so that most of the farmland and some buildings were leased to a neighbour at a small rent. In 1536, the friary was dissolved by Henry VIII and it subsequently developed into a fully-fledged farm. Even as late as 1742, when it was sketched by the Buck brothers, substantial remains survived, including the dormitory with a chimney for the 'warming room' and the chapter house, but most of the church had been lost.

Today, the friary has been completely absorbed in a large farm – Plas Newydd or Abbey farm – and the remains are visible in the farmhouse itself, but mainly in the farm-walls, hedges and the barn. Fenton, in 1810, said that 'in all the hedges and walls there are blocks of masonry and mouldings of doors and window frames everywhere'. However, the clearest archaeological evidence today are the stone monuments still surviving in the farmyard walls.

They include a stone to William Fresney, a French-speaking Archbishop, who had been a missionary preacher in the Middle East during the Crusades. He is named as the Archbishop of Edessa in south-east Turkey and shown with his mitre, a crook and a chasuble or sleeveless gown, which are all symbols of his high office. There is also an effigy of a 13th Century knight with dagger, belt and sword and now well preserved in a niche in the wall. These memorials show the importance of the Dominicans in the Crusades during the 13th Century and confirm the importance of their Friary at Rhuddlan.

Stone Statue – Rhuddlan Friary.

9. FAR FROM THE HAUNTS OF MEN
VALLE CRUCIS AND TIR-YR-ABAD

Valle Crucis is one of the finest small medieval monasteries in Britain. Much of the abbey is so well preserved that it is possible to imagine what it was like as a place where monks lived and worked eight hundred years ago. Much of the church has survived, especially the west front, the west door, the rose window and an inscription at the top of the gable-end. There are enough stumps of the pillars inside the church to identify the nave, the transepts and the chancel. Adjoining the church on its south side, the individual rooms are well preserved – the vestry (where the vestments were hung), the sacristy (where the chalice and plate were kept), a library, the chapter house and the dormitory, now freshly-roofed with Welsh slate. The abbey was founded in 1201 by Cistercian monks, part of a monastic order established at Citeaux in France and then spreading rapidly throughout Western Europe. St Bernard had become the abbot at Citeaux in 1112 and gave them a strict code of practice and an organization which gave them great success. They were willing to set up their houses in remote,

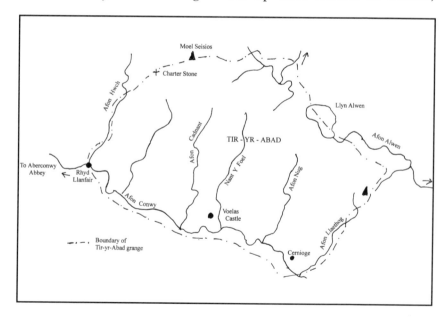

unpopulated areas 'far from the haunts of men'. Their success in Wales was also due to their willingness to accept the welcome given by the Welsh princes who, in the 12th Century, were actively opposed to the waves of Norman penetration and the setting up of castles in the lowlands and valleys. The Welsh princes were anxious to hold on to the remote moorland and mountains, and so encouraged the Cistercians to settle in these areas. They were also opposed to the establishment of churches in the Norman-held areas and the setting up of a parish system. The first monastery was built at Whitland in south-west Wales and then 'colonies' were established in central Wales and spread northwards to Valle Crucis and Aberconwy. In 1201 Madog, Prince of Powys, gave land to the Cistercians in a valley near Llangollen for the building of Valle Crucis Abbey.

The main concern in the setting up of a 'colony' was to find a place flat enough to build a church and the associated buildings to house twelve monks under the rule of an abbot. They would need land to farm and therefore buildings for the lay-brothers (the conversii), who lived separately from the monks and did the manual work. This enabled the monks to lead a life of prayer, worship and study. They also needed a source of fresh well-water, a stream to fill a well-stocked fish-pond, pasture for sheep and cattle and stone for building to be near at hand. These conditions were all met in the flood-plain of the Eglwyseg river under the shadow of Dinas Brân castle. Later on, as they became more powerful, control of bridges and ferries and mills gave them an extra income from the incoming tolls. One of the great attractions of Wales was the extensive hill pasture and moorland, especially useful for grazing sheep in summer and within easy commuting distance from the abbey. These upland granges could be worked by the lay-brothers who, unlike the monks, were not tied to a rigorous daily life of prayer from midnight in the abbey church. Some small chapels were built for the lay-brothers in the upland granges. An old chapel called 'Hen Eglwys' (Old Church) and marked in O.S. maps in the 1880's, may be a survival from this time – a substantial building is recorded in 1913. These remains have now completely disappeared, but an 'ancient' yew tree gives a clue to its site. Also it lies near Hafod yr Abad (summer pasture of the Abbot), which lies on the route to the deep valley of Valle Crucis centuries before the splendid modern route of the Horseshoe Pass.

When all the conditions of a good site had been met, the work ethic of the Cistercians gave them complete self-sufficiency in food and clothing. The abbot was accountable to the abbey at Citeaux, where he paid his annual visit. This central organization was important in the success of the Cistercian order; Citeaux would provide support, plans, money and masons so that the resulting monasteries were the same except for size and the constraints of the site. Masons' marks in their stonework show that masons moved from site to site.

After founding Whitland (1140) they had, by 1200, established monasteries at Valle Crucis, Cymer near Dolgellau, Aberconwy and, with Basingwerk, completed their colonization of northern Wales. All the 'old' counties of northern Wales, except Anglesey, had a Cistercian house. The Welsh princes at this time were strong and largely independent of England. Llywelyn ap Iorwerth (Llywelyn the Great) exercised authority throughout most of Wales from his capital, Aberffraw, in Anglesey. He gave permission to the Cistercians to build at typical riverside sites at Cymer and Aberconwy (in 1198), granting a detailed charter in Latin giving details of grants of land in the remote mountains of Gwynedd, where his power was complete. A fine example of one of these granges is known as 'Tir yr Abad' (Land of the Abbot) from near Pentrefoelas to Aberconwy Abbey. It was a good day's walk from the monastery, but provided good summer grazing for sheep in an area mainly above 1000 feet. Although the Charter was written in Latin – the language of the monks – the place-names are in Welsh and were given phonetically to the monks, who did their best to write them down accurately. Some of these 12th Century place-names can still be clearly identified on O.S. maps today; some names are uncertain, some can be guessed, but there are enough which can be recognized, so that the boundary of this grange can be plotted. At a day's distance from the abbey, the lay-brothers tended the sheep – lambing, shearing – with occasional visits from the monks to supervise sales of wool and marketing records. The

Valle Crucis Abbey.
Centre – door to Chapter House; Left – iron-framed library;
Right – door to stairs leading to dormitory; Dormitory windows – above.

boundary of Tir yr Abad started at Rhydlanfair on the River Conwy – Cistercian churches were called 'Llanfair' – a dedication to Mary. The boundary then followed Afon Hwch to the summit of Moel Seisiog, passing the 'Charter Stone' (Maen Satyr) and crossing into the Alwen valley. It then followed the Alwen river and through Llyn Alwen, along Afon Llaethog (called Llaethnauc in 1198) into Afon Nug. It then followed the Afon Nug and returned along the Conwy river to Rhydlanfair. Tir yr Abad continued to be Cistercian-owned land until 1536 when Henry VIII dissolved the monasteries. The land then fell into the hands of the descendants of a local war-lord (Rhys ap Meredudd) who had assisted the Tudors (Henry VII) at the Battle of Bosworth (1485). They became officials of Henry VIII and, later, Elizabeth and their fine houses at Foelas, Cernioge, Plas Iolyn and Gilar testify to their wealth and importance.

The upland grange may have been a valuable outpost of the abbey but the heart of the day-to-day organization was the Chapter House. It was situated next to the Vestry and Sacristy – where the vestments and sacred vessels were kept – on the south side of the South Transept of the Church. From its single-arched door it looked out on to the central courtyard or cloister. Next to the Chapter House on the south side, was the parlour or passage where the monks were allowed conversations, which were otherwise forbidden by the rule of silence. The Chapter House was the busy hub of life; each morning the monks collected here for a reading by one of their members, a chapter of the rule of St Bernard, and hence the name 'Chapter House'. The monks would be dressed in tunics of undyed wool (the 'White Monks') and black shoulder-width scapular. During the rest of the day, the Chapter House would be used for business and administration. The monks would confess their failings and misdemeanours to the abbot and receive punishment. Visiting abbots and bishops would hold inquiries here and it was the room for dealing with rents and the management and accounts of the abbey and the granges.

The importance of the Chapter House was shown in the design and architecture; it was always a square room of imposing construction. The walls were made of dressed stone and, at Valle Crucis, the stone seats around the edges of the room survive. The most striking feature are the pillars, evenly spaced, which carry the weight of the roof and dormitory above. The strength and beauty of these rib-vaults is one of the finest surviving features of Valle Crucis. In some cases, these vault-shafts had bosses, which still retain the red paint and gilding, which would have been a spectacular sight when sunlight streamed in through the three east-facing windows. Apart from the wall-seats, there was a lectern for reading the chapter and there were wooden benches and tables where business matters could be dealt with.

From its central position in the abbey plan, the Chapter House had easy access to the vestry and the church as well as the cloisters, kitchen and dining room. Next door, at Valle Crucis, a small pointed doorway opens onto a narrow winding staircase set in the thickness of the walls. This lead to the comfortable dormitory for the monks and the abbot's lodging on the first floor.

10. A SANCTUARY-RING
IN THE BELFRY TOWER
MEDIEVAL CAERWYS

Caerwys is first recorded as 'Cairos' in the Domesday Book (1086) and was noted there as an area of farmland with one plough, a serf (landless) and six peasants working the open-fields. There was also a sizeable belt of woodland – on the slopes east and west – and the 'manor' was worth 15 shillings. There was nothing in Domesday to make it distinguishable from the rest of the small hamlets with their open fields and pasture in north-central Flintshire. Only twenty years after the Norman conquest of England, the area was dominated by the new town of Rhuddlan. Here there was a motte and bailey castle, a church, mills, fisheries, an iron mine and even a mint for producing short-cross silver pennies. The town's value is recorded in Domesday as £3.

By contrast, Caerwys was probably a few mud-walled cottages with small allotments for working the land around the wooden church of St Michael's. In 1249, a letter from the Pope mentions Caerwys as a meeting-place for an arbitration by the abbots of Aberconwy and Cymer on a Treaty between Prince Dafydd and Henry III to determine its fairness and legality. The area was subsequently fought over during the 1270's and early 1280's when Edward I overran Flintshire and built large stone castles at Flint and Rhuddlan. The Welsh Prince had a residence at Maes Maenan near Caerwys and it is likely that the church at Caerwys was damaged. In 1284, there is a reference to the church when compensation was paid to the Rector – Gervase – by Edward I for damage done by his soldiers during the war.

With the conquest of northern Wales completed in 1284, Edward may have had a 'soft spot' for Caerwys because he granted it a Royal Charter, which made it a free borough. It made the men of Caerwys free burgesses with narrow burgage plots laid out, a merchants' guild, a trading house (hanse) and all the liberties to trade exactly similar to those granted in his new castle-towns of Flint and Rhuddlan. Apart from Caerwys, all the newly planted

The 13th Century Tower and
The North Aisle at Caerwys church.

Sanctuary knocker on an inner door to
the Belfry Tower – Caerwys church.

towns – ten in northern Wales – had castles. Caerwys was to be a trading town – a 'bastide de commerce' – without a castle and defensive town walls. The other feature was that the new liberties were given to the Welsh native population and not the incoming English settlers. The town was laid out in a rectangular plan with two main streets intersecting at the centre where the market square was situated. The church was rebuilt in stone in the Late Decorative Style in 1292 and a list of all the burgesses who lived in its shadow was recorded in vellum. Using local limestone, the massive church tower was built and the two naves were similar to the contemporary churches in the neighbouring Vale of Clwyd and also Treuddyn and Cilcain. The church is attributed to the Bishop of St Asaph, Anian II, who held the diocese from 1268 until 1292 and was responsible for building a number of these double-nave churches. Anian had accompanied Edward I as his Confessor on a Crusade to the Holy Land, and almost all the existing churches in northern Flintshire had to be rebuilt after Edward's Conquest. Anian had been a Dominican friar and the double-nave was a feature of the Dominican mother church at Toulouse. Anian had been Prior at the Dominican friary at nearby Rhuddlan (now known as 'Abbey Farm') and acted as an intermediary between the Welsh and English during the war. It is recorded that Dominican friars at Rhuddlan took charge of the English soldiers of Edward I, wounded during the earlier skirmishes of 1277. This may have influenced Edward I in his dealings with the rebuilding of Caerwys church and the favoured status as a trading town given to Caerwys. In the taxatio Ecclesiasticus of Pope Nicholas, made in 1291 for recording taxation, the church is referred to as 'Caerwys'.

During the 14th and 15th Centuries Caerwys continued to prosper as the only market town of Flintshire benefitting from its position near the Chester-Rhuddlan road and the sales of sheep and cattle. This prosperity is shown by the inscribed stone slabs which are the memorial stones of the rich merchants now mounted on the inside walls of the church tower. This link is also shown, even as late as Elizabethan times, by the tombstone of the 'Boy Rector' which can be seen in the south wall outside the church. He was Robert Evans, son of a rich merchant, and the stone memorial, in Latin, reads:

HIC IACET ROBERT EVANS DE CAIRWIS.
SEPULTUS. 13.DIE. AUGUST. ANNO
DOMINE. 1582
HERE LIES ROBERT EVANS OF CAERWYS
DIED 13TH AUGUST 1582

He had been rector of Caerwys since 1557 and died at the age of 34.

The most impressive feature of the church is still the Tower. The limestone walls with slit windows rise to the projecting ridge just below the clock, and is the original structure completed in 1290. The ridge was once the coping of the top of the medieval tower, with evidence provided by the gargoyles projecting from the corners. The upper storey, with its 'false' battlements, was added in the late 17th Century with a beam in the Bell-Tower dated 1687. In the Belfry there is a medieval 'Sanctus Bell' (Priest's Bell) with contemporary Latin Lombardic lettering which reads:

+ CAMPANA MICHAELIS

Inside the church, apart from the coffin lids, there is an effigy in the sanctuary beneath a finely-carved canopy. This is the effigy of Elizabeth, wife of Dafydd, the last Prince of Wales. From the late 13th Century to the early 15th Century, effigies were common in churches in northern Wales, carved from limestone and Gwespyr sandstone from a 'school' of stonemasons in north Flintshire. It is thought that Elizabeth died a few years earlier than Dafydd (d.1282) and was buried here.

Another medieval relic is the Sanctuary Ring, which is in the old door of the Belfry Tower and is probably the only one still existing in Wales. It recalls the right of sanctuary, which was one of the sanctions held by the powerful medieval church. The tradition was that if a fugitive took hold of the sanctuary ring before being caught he had freedom from prosecution for forty days. Some fugitives hoped to secure a pardon whilst they were still protected by the right of sanctuary. Sometimes the criminal donned sackcloth and was escorted to the nearest port and then left the country. In Wales, according to Gerald the Welshman writing in 1190, 'the churches were quiet and more tranquil than elsewhere'. The boundaries of sanctuary extended from the yew tree by the gate to the church door. These sanctuary limits were fixed by the bishop and it was not even necessary to get inside the church. In Durham Cathedral, the bronze knocker on its broad north door is a grotesque lion's head, which has lost its enamel eyes, but the great ring gave welcome sanctuary to anyone who grasped it. A book in the Cathedral records that 331 criminals sought refuge there between 1464 and 1534 and that most of them were murderers. In the late Middle Ages, as the power of the Catholic Church waned, so the rights of sanctuary were challenged by the King. In 1529, in the reign of Henry VIII, it was enacted that those who had entered sanctuary for felony or murder should be branded on the right thumb, and by 1540 sanctuary was abolished altogether except for those charged with murder, rape and burglary. In 1623, James II virtually abolished it although, occasionally, well into the 19th Century, sanctuary was granted to those in debt. The Sanctuary Ring in the Belfry-Tower door at Caerwys reminds us of the days of an all-powerful church.

Even as late as 1848, when the Tithe Map of Caerwys was drawn, the town still retained its medieval origins. The map shows the rectangular lay-out, the two main streets intersecting at the market square – indicated by a tree – the gardens and allotments that had originally belonged to the 43 burgesses. The importance of the church is shown by the glebe land (rector's field), which occupied almost one quarter of the town area. The houses still retained their frontages on the main streets and the town was almost exactly contained within its medieval boundaries.

Ascending the spiral staircase in the wall of the church tower would have demanded steady nerves and carefully placed feet. It is a narrow, steep, winding ascent in almost claustrophobic darkness and the medieval bell-ringers would have needed good eye-sight with only candle-light to guide them. Today the door to the Bell-Tower is kept firmly locked.

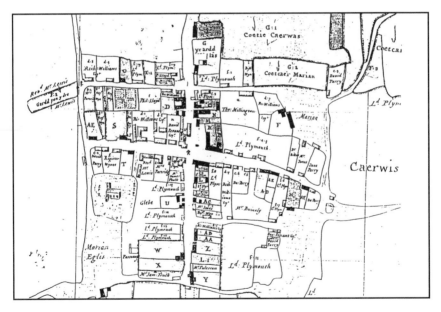

Estate Map of Caerwys (1747) showing the survival of the medieval town-plan.

11. DRAMA ON THE SHORE
THE SCENE OF RICHARD II'S AMBUSH
AT PENMAEN-RHOS

In the autumn of 1399, Richard II made an expedition to Ireland from Milford Haven. He was in Dublin when he received news that his sworn enemy, Henry Bolingbroke, who had been banished, had returned to England and that his claim to the throne was supported by most of the powerful nobles. The King sent his chief supporter, the Earl of Salisbury, to Conwy to gather an army of 40,000 men. With the exception of a hundred of these, whose loyalty was to Salisbury, most of the army deserted when they realized that Richard was still in Ireland and that the outcome with Bolinbroke was uncertain. The King returned to Milford Haven and with thirteen bodyguards set out for Conwy which they reached in thirty hours of hard riding. They arrived at daybreak and quietly passed through the narrow gates of the town and entered the safety of the hundred-year old castle on the banks of the river Conwy. Richard, who was uncertain of his rival's plans, soon left for Beaumaris castle and then Caernarfon castle, but here the shortage

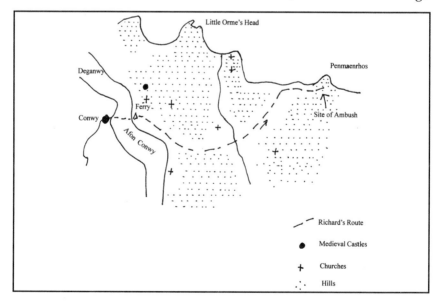

of food and the inadequate accommodation (he slept on the floor on bare straw) persuaded him to return to the comfortable royal apartments at Conwy castle. It was perhaps on this return journey, with a small retinue of nobles and bodyguards taking an easier route over the hills to avoid the rocky headland and vertical cliffs of Penmaenmawr, that one of the party lost a gold coin which was a contemporary half-noble of Richard II himself. This coin was found in a garden in Llanfairfechan in 1894 and may have been part of a coin-hoard hidden by an anxious King and his party. It is believed to have been washed down from Garreg Fawr, which is a prominent ridge above the village, in the great flood of 1873. The track along the grass slopes north of the rocky outcrops of Garreg Fawr would have been the most likely route for Richard and his followers on their way from Caernarfon to Conwy. Even today, the rain-washed pastures of Garreg Fawr provide rich fodder for wild horses.

Bolingbroke had, by this time, reached Chester and sent an emissary – Henry Percy, the Earl of Northumberland – who promised to bring Richard to Chester 'by reason or craft'. On his way to Conwy, Percy left some of his men in a prepared ambush site under the 'rough and lofty cliffs' of Penmaen-rhos whilst he continued to Conwy. He claimed that Bolingbroke would request a pardon if Richard restored him as Chief Judge of England and gave him authority to try some of the Earls who had supported Richard. The King agreed to these terms at a solemn mass by the Archbishop of Canterbury and the Earl of Northumberland in the Garrison Chapel at Conwy castle. Richard was confident that he could eventually outwit Bolingbroke and put him to death. The King persuaded the Earl of Northumberland to go ahead to Rhuddlan castle and make arrangements for dinner. Northumberland then left Conwy and made his way to the prepared ambush site, where his men were still waiting. In the King's retinue there was a French nobleman – Jean Creton – who left a detailed account of Richard's subsequent journey following Northumberland to the ambush site, so it is possible to work out the precise location of the site and the route taken. Creton had come over from France in 1399 'for amusement' and to see the country and became caught up in the events leading to the overthrow of Richard by Bolingbroke. On his return home, he wrote an account of what he had seen, in order to shame Richard's enemies.

According to Creton's eye-witness account, the King left the castle at Conwy and 'passed a broad and great water' – the Conwy estuary – to the opposite bank and 'then rode for four miles' until he mounted the rock where the Earl (of Northumberland) was concealed at the descent'. Four, or perhaps, five miles would have taken the King to the limestone headland of Penmaen-rhos. On his eastward descent of this headland, the King took a broad stony path from the clifftop down to the eastern hollow, where the ambush was to be sprung. (This track still exists today and has a 'primitive' appearance ending at the point where the railway enters a tunnel). The King, on seeing the banners of the Earl of Northumberland, realized that 'he was in such a place that he (the King) could not escape'. Despite the solemn oath taken at Conwy castle, he had been betrayed, and could not evade capture. 'The sea beating on one side and the rock keeping him in on the other; and if he should have fled back, they would have caught him before he could reach Conwy for he had only twenty-three men in his company'. The King, therefore, descended the track and the Earl knelt before him and promised that his men were there only to protect the King. The King mentioned that only six bodyguards were needed and that he would go back to Conwy. Northumberland refused and told the King that he would lead him to Bolingbroke as promised. He offered the King bread and wine and then the King remounted his horse and rode on to Rhuddlan castle. Here they 'dined sumptuously at the castle' and then went on to spend the night at Flint castle, awaiting a decision to go on to Chester to meet Bolingbroke.

The route taken by Richard II followed a well-used road and track used since the occupation of Wales (1282) to link the royal castles at Rhuddlan and Conwy. Records for 1281-2 show that wages were paid to men for building the road and that carts were used to carry the Queen's baggage from Rhuddlan to Conwy. From Conwy, a ferry operated to the opposite bank of the estuary and had earlier provided handsome tolls to the monks of Aberconwy

Dolos units below ambush site

before the castle was built. From the ferry house, the road then ran along the wide valley to Mochdre and then across the low hills to the coast at Colwyn Bay. The road then climbed the headland of Penmaen-rhos and descended as a rocky, winding track to reach the coast on the eastern side of the cliffs. It was when Richard II descended this slope that he realized that he was trapped with no way to escape. The headland had vertical cliffs with the tide flowing across flat rocks and shingle to sea-caves at its extremity. In later times, (1624), there is a reference to the need to repair the road above and below Penmaen-rhos. A letter, dated 19 May, 1624, from Sir Roger Mostyn to his father-in-law, Sir John Wynn of Gwydir castle, asks his father-in-law to 'give Evan Jones charge to mend the way both above and under Penmayn for a coach, lest the weather be foul so that if they may not take one way they may take the other'. There exists today a broad stony path from the cliff top to the eastern hollow where the railway tunnel begins. This is all that remains of the coach road which is referred to in Sir Roger's letter.

These cliffs continued to deter travellers until the end of the 18th Century; 'it was so formidably narrow and unprotected that few people dare trust themselves or their horses upon it'. At this time, Dr Johnson said that 'to spare the horrors of Penmaen-rhos, we sent the coach over the road cross the mountain . . . I, with Mr Thale, walked along the edge of the cliff face where the path is very narrow and much encumbered by little loose stones which had fallen down since we passed before'. Two years later, in 1776, another traveller, Cradlock, claimed that Penmaen-rhos 'was by far the worst part of the road between Holyhead and Chester'.

Today, this perilous track along the seaward edge of Penmaen-rhos has been replaced by a dual carriageway (A55) which runs smoothly along a ledge above the old shoreline, but a wide zone of 22,000 stone blocks (dolos units) protects it from the sea. Despite these changes, the medieval ambush site can still be clearly seen near the tunnel where Northumberland's men-at-arms lurked to ambush Richard II.

History records that Richard died imprisoned in Pontefract castle in 1400, probably murdered by starvation on the orders of Henry Bolingbroke, now Henry IV. Henry went to great lengths to broadcast the news of Richard's death and a parade of the body was set up from Pontefract to Westminster, stopping at every important town, to display the face to crowds of onlookers. The body was buried at a remote spot at King's Langley, Hertfordshire, to prevent a cult developing around the deposed King. Rumours persisted that, disguised as a monk, he had fled to Scotland to Stirling castle, where he died later and was buried under the altar of the Church of the Black Friars.

Half-noble coin of Richard II found in Llanfairfechan.

12. PILGRIMAGE TO LLANDDERFEL
DERFEL'S HORSE AT LLANDDERFEL CHURCH

Few people today visit the quiet village of Llandderfel in the Upper Dee valley, but in 1538, between five and six hundred people were reported to have visited the church of St Derfel in one day. St Derfel is a mysterious Celtic Saint or Missionary who lived in the Sixth Century A.D. and is thought to have come from Brittany to spread Christianity in Wales. This is the only dedication to the Saint in northern Wales but there is another church dedicated to him in southern Wales. There are many references to him in southern Wales. There are also many references to him in Welsh medieval poetry, where he is always depicted as 'Derfel Gadarn' – Derfel the Mighty. He is reputed to have taken part in the famous battle of Camlan in which King Arthur was killed. The exact location of Camlan in Snowdonia is unknown, but claims have been made for a site between Dolgellau and Mallwyd, where the name survives in three separate places. Another site suggested is near Pentrefoelas, where forty stone graves dating to the 6th Century – including a chief, Brohmagli and his wife Caune – were uncovered when

Llandderfel church – remains of Derfel's horse .

Dr Ellis Price (Prys)
of Plas Iolyn, Pentrefoelas.
(portrait in Mostyn Hall)

Telford's road (now the A5) was being constructed. Forty graves in a small area suggests the aftermath of an important battle which took place in the 'Dark Ages'.

Unlike Arthur, Derfel survived the battle and in poetry, written in the 13th and 14th Century, based on oral traditions, he is depicted as a warrior in full armour accompanied by a red stag. He became the object of a cult in the later Middle Ages, which was focussed on the church dedicated to him at Llandderfel. Other associations near the village include Ffynnon Derfel, a well on the nearby Garn y Llan hill – which had famous healing waters – and Bryn Saint, which is a field behind the Rectory. These are archaeological features and place-names which record the life and importance of St Derfel. However, in the 15th-16th Century, the cult was based on a wooden figure of a knight in full armour mounted on a horse or stag in the church itself.

In the early 16th Century, in the reign of Henry VIII, a curb on lawless bandits in northern Wales had at last given a measure of security that encouraged a revival of interest in travel and pilgrimages. The devout and physically fit were able to test their faith by visiting places where the Celtic Saints had lived or where some relic of their lives had survived. Holy wells dedicated to the Celtic Saints and near the old churches were a particular draw and had acquired reputations for healing and cures. The all-powerful Catholic Church had nurtured these holy wells and shrines and in a 'league table' of pilgrimages, two visits to St David's in Pembrokeshire was equal to one visit to Rome. A visit to Bardsey Island was equally important and many medieval Christians chose to be buried on Bardsey. The pilgrim road passed through Clynnog

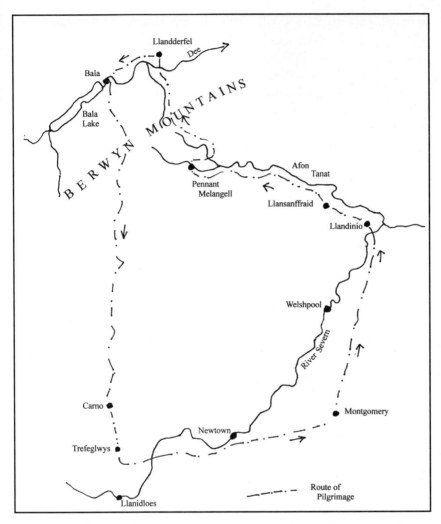

Fawr, which was the most important stopping point for Bardsey-bound pilgrims. Here, the church of St Beuno contained St Beuno's chapel – Capel y Bedd – underneath which ancient masonry was found in 1913, which dated to the 7th Century and may be the foundations of the first cell of St Beuno, the main Celtic Saint in northern Wales. The holy well still survives and was used for healing until the 18th Century. In Holywell, St Winifred's Well was reputed to effect miraculous cures and was the principal attraction in north-eastern Wales, where the infirm pilgrims were happy to immerse themselves in the cold waters of the chapel well. The money which the pilgrims brought helped to restore churches and even pay for the finest stained-glass windows. The best example in northern Wales is the famous Jesse Window at Llanrhaeadr in the Vale of Clwyd, which was paid for by pilgrims visiting the shrine and well of St Dyrnog. Of the many churches in northern Wales, the most favoured by pilgrims was St Derfel's at Llandderfel. Money contributed by pilgrims paid for the rebuilding of the church in 1500, with its fine east window. The richly carved rood-screen which separates the chancel and the nave is one of the finest in northern Wales and also dates to this period. The pilgrims, however, came to see and touch the imposing wooden image of St Derfel – a medieval life-size carving of the saint in armour mounted on his horse and proudly displayed in the church.

At this time an important landowner in neighbouring Montgomeryshire – Sir Morgan Herbert – mentions the pilgrimage site at Llandderfel in his will. In the will, dated 19th July 1526, he states that his servant, Hywel Gethin, 'shall have my gown of black cloth and he shall go on certain pilgrimages for me, that is to say, to Llandrinio, Llansantffraid, Pennant Melangell, Llandderfel, Carno and Trefeglwys and at each place to offer four pence'. This arduous route of pilgrimage would have involved at least seventy miles – mainly along uncertain mountain paths – to visit all the isolated churches mentioned in the will. The most isolated was the famous shrine of St Melangell – which still survives – in the beautiful Cwm Pennant valley, west of Llangynog. From here, Hywel Gethin would go by mountain track over the formidable Berwyn Range where bandits and outlaws were still active. When he reached the furthest point of his pilgrimage at Llandderfel, he would be only one of many pilgrims at St Derfel's shrine in 1526, when the cult was at its height. But shortly afterwards, Henry VIII had broken the power of the Catholic church in England and Wales and by 1536, had dissolved the monasteries mainly through the authority and planning of his chief minister, Thomas Cromwell. Attention was then turned to shrines and steps were taken to abrogate cults and pilgrimage sites. Thomas Cromwell appointed the notorious Dr Ellis Price as Commissioner of the Diocese of St Asaph to look into 'images abused by superstitious rites'. His main concern was the statue of 'Mighty Derfel', which was only eight miles from Ellis Price's mansion at Plas Iolyn near Cerrigydrudion. Ellis Price wrote a letter to Cromwell on April 6th 1538 that said 'there is an image of Derfel Gadarn, in whom people have so great confidence, hope and trust that they come daily on a pilgrimage, some with cattle, others with oxen and horses and the rest with money. There were five and six hundred pilgrims, to a man's estimation, that offered to the said image on the 15th day of April, 1538 which is the Feast Day of St Derfel'.

Cromwell ordered that the statue was to be taken to London. A further letter from Ellis Price to Cromwell said that he had been offered forty shillings by the vicar and parishioners to keep the statue in Llandderfel and that the priest and 'others' were heading for London to demand the return of their famous statue. On 2nd May 1538, the statue of St Derfel ended up at Smithfield in London; it was carried by eight men and placed on the pyre which consumed the body of Sir John Forrest, a friar, who had denied Henry VIII's authority over the Roman Catholic Church. The porch at Llandderfel church, however, still retains the wooden image of an animal lying down with its legs tucked under the body. It originally stood in the north sanctuary of the church and with the life-size figure of the Saint in armour would have been a very imposing statue. Damage to the horse or stag in later centuries have diminished it, but it is still an unique wooden relic and a reminder of the power of religion in the later Middle Ages.

13. BANDIT PATHS FOR THE ROYAL MAP-MAKER
CHRISTOPHER SAXTON'S MAPS

It was a rare treat a few years ago to see Christopher Saxton's superb original map of Caernarfon and Anglesey published in 1578, and for sale in an antique map and print shop in Chester. The map could be identified as a genuine original from its printer's mark, a plate-edge just outside the frame of the map and a watermark. Four centuries of wear and tear had exposed a small fragment of the original linen on which the map had been printed. The maps of Wales each cover two counties and the Chester dealer had recently sold a Meirionnydd-Montgomery map by Saxton for £850 to an American buyer.

Christopher Saxton was born in a small hamlet near Dewsbury in West Yorkshire in 1544 and was educated at Wakefield Grammar School and, later, Cambridge University. According to a contemporary record he was skilled in Geometry and competent in surveying. He travelled throughout England and Wales from 1574

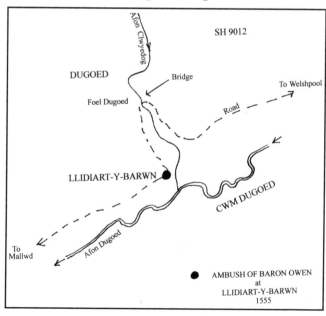

and drew all the counties of England separately and had them engraved on bronze plates to be issued as maps on cloth or vellum. It is thought that in this work he was strongly influenced by John Rudd, Vicar of Dewsbury, who had a consuming interest in cartography and travelled extensively throughout England. Rudd's interest is shown by the fact that he was granted leave from his church to travel. A receipt dated 1570 was signed by Saxton when he visited Durham to collect Rudd's stipend. One of the great mysteries about Saxton is the speed with which he completed his survey and maps at a time when road travel was difficult and dangerous. It is possible that his close connection with Rudd in the early 1570's gave him extensive training in the methods of surveying and he may even have collected material for his maps at this time.

One fact is certain – he was chosen by Thomas Seckford of Woodbridge in Suffolk to survey the counties of England and Wales and he financed this great undertaking. Seckford was M.P. for Ipswich, was also a wealthy landowner and had close connections with William Cecil, who was the principal adviser to Queen Elizabeth throughout her reign. Saxton started his survey in 1574 in Suffolk and then travelled as far as Cornwall and later extended his travels to the north of England. He finished his survey of Wales in 1578 and published his entire work as an Atlas in 1579; this was the first Atlas covering the whole of England and Wales. William Cecil took great interest in the progress of the survey and Saxton sent him the maps for engraving. The Queen gave Saxton the licence to print the maps and her Coat of Arms appears on each map. The Queen's authority to carry out the survey was vitally important and she required local officials – magistrates and J.P.'s – in all parts of Wales to assist him in his requirements. This was important because in the remoter part of Wales, law and order had only just been secured. Thomas Seckford persuaded the Privy Council to grant Saxton special privileges for his work; he was 'to be assisted in all places where he shall come for the view of such places, to describe certain counties in maps'. Anticipating special difficulties in Wales, an order was sent to all mayors and Justices of the Peace in Wales instructing them 'to see him conducted to any tower, castle, high place or hill to view the county, and that he be accompanied by two or three honest men such as do best know the county for the better accomplishment of that service; and that at his departure from any town or place that he hath taken views of the said town do set forth a horseman that can speak both English and Welsh to safe conduct him to the next market town'.

His chief method was to climb a church tower, castle or prominent hill and, with local assistance, he would take bearings on the main villages and was then told their names. This local knowledge gave great accuracy to this new survey, which was extended to include names of rivers, lakes, mountains and some coastal features such as islands and headlands.

The resulting map of Wales shows most of the villages and towns, though there is a greater wealth of detail in those areas which were easier to map. A notable example is Anglesey with its many closely-spaced churches, its flatness and the many hills gives it the largest number of named villages. It was a pre-industrial period so that the map of northern Wales is dominated by villages and small market towns. The largest towns such as Flint, Bangor and Denbigh are shown in capital letters and the map is a reasonable guide to the geography of Elizabethan northern Wales. The coastline is reasonably accurate and shows headlands such as the Great Orme, straits such as the Menai Strait and islands such as St Tudwal's and Priestholme. Most of the rivers are named and can often be traced to their sources deep in the mountains. Many of the lakes are shown and named – Llyn Tryweryn in the wilds of the Migneint, Llyn Aled in the heart of the Mynydd Hiraethog and even Llyn Bychan in the Rhinogydd. This attention to detail is unexpected for the period and makes the maps interesting and readable even today.

At this time, travel was done on horseback on roads – apart from those linking the medieval castle towns – which were merely beaten trackways without a permanent all-weather surface. The main mountain areas of Snowdonia and Cader Idris were inaccessible and impenetrable. Saxton did not venture into these areas and depended on second-hand information about them. The

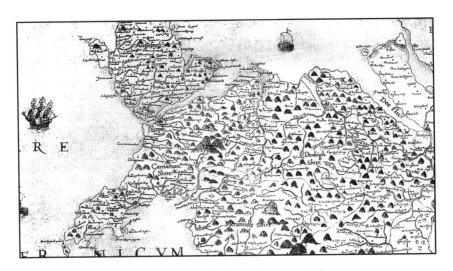

Christopher Saxton's Map of northern Wales.

only lake shown in or near Cader Idris is Tal-y-llyn which lies in an open easily accessible valley, whereas the magnificent mountain lakes such as Llyn Cau and Llyn y Gadair are not shown. Another major difficulty facing Saxton was that law and order had only recently been established in some remote districts and these areas were still dangerous. A very forbidding area was centred on Dinas Mawddwy and Mallwyd in the deeply-cut, wooded valleys of the Dyfi headwaters in Merioneth. The Dugoed valley, east of Mallwyd, was inhabited by the 'Gwylliad Cochion Mawddwy' – the 'Red Bandits of Mawddwy'. They lived in large numbers on the slopes of Moel y Dugoed – the Great Dark Wood. A letter written about 1775 says that 'they built no houses, and practised but few of the arts of civilized life. They possessed great powers over the arrow and the stone, and never missed their mark. They had a chief and kept together in the most tenacious manner, having but little contact with the surrounding neighbourhood, except in the way of plundering; they would not hesitate to drive away sheep and cattle in large numbers to their dens'. To put a stop to this tribal lawlessness a commission was granted to Baron Lewis Owen of Dolgellau, who was the Baron of the Exchequer of northern Wales, to confront them. He raised a body of strong armed men on

Christmas Eve 1554 and seized about a hundred of the 'Gwylliaid' and these was hanged and buried in a mound in the Dugoed valley in an attempt to stamp out this anarchy. The surviving tribesmen determined to avenge the onslaught, and revenge came swiftly in 1555. Baron Owen, on his way to the Montgomeryshire Assizes, had to pass through the Dugoed forest on his way to Welshpool. In a narrow, wooded ravine the bandits cut down several tall trees to block the road and impede his passage. They discharged a shower of arrows and then attacked Baron Owen with hooks and javelins and left him dead at the ambush site, which is now re-called by the place-name 'Llidiart y Barwn' – the Gate of the Baron. His death gave peace to the area after soldiers were sent to exterminate and disperse the bandits. This event survived in the memory of the local population and was referred to over two hundred years later when Thomas Pennant visited the area. 'I was told that the bandits were so feared that travellers did not dare to go along the common road to Shrewsbury, but passed over the summits of the mountains to avoid the haunts of the bandits. The inhabitants placed scythes in the chimneys of their house to prevent felons coming down to surprise them at night; some of which are to be seen to this (1778) day'. The common road is now the A458, which crosses the wooded ravine at Llidiart y Barwn in a dramatic hair-pin bend and, further downstream, the 'Brigands Inn' at Mallwyd also recalls these events.

Another 'no-go' area was the neighbouring Berwyn Mountains, which, in the mid-16th century, was also infamous for its outlaws. This fact may explain why Saxton did not venture into this area and did not show the Berwyn Mountains on his map. The river Ceiriog, which is shown on his map, has its source in the High Berwyn, but its course is not accurately shown. The important village of Llanarmon Dyffryn Ceiriog is not even shown on the river and this suggests that Saxton did not personally visit the area.

Despite all these problems, Saxton completed his survey of Wales and all the maps were printed in 1579. He was the 'Father of Cartography' of England and Wales and his Atlas remains a formidable expression of the attitude and spirit of the Elizabethan Age.

14. 'PEACE TO THIS HOUSE'
CRUCK-FRAMED HOUSES

In the later Middle Ages, in the dense oak forests of the West Midlands of England, permanent domestic buildings for the emerging farming class began to be built in large numbers. The method was to select a strong oak tree – up to a hundred years old – using the trunk and a convenient bough, which were then split in half. The trunk and bough were sawn lengthwise into two identical blades to form a matching pair or couple called a 'cruck'. The bough was placed downwards on the ground or on a sill in the wall so that the trunk supported the massive ridge roof. From the 13th Century onwards, until the 17th Century, this method became common along the Welsh Border and spread into the forested valleys of northern Wales, and even into the stone areas of Snowdonia. These cruck-framed houses and barns have survived in Flintshire, around Wrexham, the Vale of Clwyd, the Ceiriog and Dee valleys. They are found in the Conwy valley, with a fine example at Hendre Wen near Betws-y-coed, which was dismantled and re-built at St Fagan's Museum in Cardiff. West of the Conwy,

Tan-y-Llan near Wrexham – a fine cruck house with gable-end external chimney.

their numbers decrease, but some are found in remote mountain valleys in Snowdonia. Cruck-framed houses are completely absent in Anglesey and Llŷn Peninsula. Later, when the farmers became more prosperous, they converted their cruck houses into barns. In specially built barns, the timbers often have the original saw marks and even the raw bark is preserved. In the farmhouses the timbers have been planed and painted over centuries of care and in the bedrooms the polished dark oak is an attractive feature today.

Cruck-building was a relatively easy method of construction in areas of plentiful oak trees; the blades were assembled on the spot where the house was to be built and they were then reared up and held together at the collar by horizontal beams. The blades were either placed at ground level in the rubble-filled foundations or were placed a few feet from the ground on stone pads in the wall itself. It would have been a satisfying sight for the farmer to see his house being built quickly and securing a house which would last his lifetime and beyond. Its essential feature was the capacity of the crucks to support the weight of the roof without the necessity of load-bearing walls. The walls would then be built of timber, wattle and daub, stone or weather-board panels. These 'new' houses replaced the thatched roof, mud-walled cottages which hardly lasted a generation. It must have been a marvellous occasion for the farmer and his family to see the cruck-frames exposed in each gable-end of the building. This distinctive architectural style has fortunately survived and the dark cruck-frames stand out against the white walls of the house.

There are practically no documents to recall the precise dating of these houses; they have no known history for this was a time when the Welsh did not use surnames so that owners and occupiers are recorded simply as 'son of' ('ap', in Welsh), as in the Bible. They were a common sight along the Welsh Borders in the 16th Century and continued to be built as barns into the 17th Century. There is some evidence that examples in northern Wales can be traced to the 14th and 15th Centuries. A good example of a cruck house still in good condition is Tan-y-Llan in Esclusham near Wrexham. It was built about 1565 to house a farmer and his family to last his lifetime and to be handed on to his children. It has

A cruck-frame surviving in an outbuilding at Ty'n-y-Celyn Farm near Waen, Bodfari.

survived well and was, at a later date, given a second storey with
dormer windows and an external chimney stack added to the
gable-end. The gable-end is otherwise unaltered and the original
crucks are exposed to give a faithful record of its construction.
There is a cluster of similar small farmhouses near Bryn Eglwys
with some polished crucks exposed in the bedrooms; other houses
in the area have evolved into barns. They were, essentially, small
farmhouses originally and are typically named 'tŷ' or 'tyddyn'
(house or small holding). This is shown by a group of closely-
spaced cruck houses near Hirwaen in the Vale of Clwyd – 'Ty'n
Dŵr', 'Tŷ Coch' and 'Tyddyn Uchaf'. An unusual case is 'Plas yn
Crwmp' near Afon Wen. As a place-name 'Plas' usually denotes a
mansion or big house and is therefore unlikely to describe a small
cruck house. 'Crwmp' may refer to the site – a hump or mound –
or the shape of the roof. It is a late-16th Century cottage, which is
considered in its class to be one of the most important structures in

Wales. In Ty'n-y-Celyn, near Bodfari, a small building which is unlikely to have been a barn, displays the original crucks which still look freshly cut timber. At Pant Glas-Uchaf, near Ruthin, the present-day barn was the original farmhouse. It was a four-bay cruck dwelling of the 15th Century which, two hundred years later, was converted into the barn. It is still a fine structure with well-preserved cruck-beams, an arch brace linking the crucks and weather-board on a stone base. It is not always necessary to go into country areas; they were also built in towns such as Ruthin. On the Mold road an extended bungalow still proudly retains the gable-end crucks and stone foundations.

An interesting aspect is the spread of cruck building into Snowdonia, where stone and slate are plentiful and would be the most suitable building materials. Just across the Denbighshire border with Caernarfonshire there is an 'outpost' of cruck design in the mountain valley of Afon Glasgwm near Penmachno. At some time in the 16th Century, a cottage – Blaen-y-Glasgwm – was built of uncoursed rubble and a boulder foundation but had two rooms with a cruck frame in each room and which are still well preserved. The crucks stand at about a metre from the floor on wall pads. The original cottage had a loft lit by skylights; a small window in the east gable still survives. In the Wynn Papers – written before 1627 – a reference to the cottage, as well as its cruck roof, suggests a 16th Century date.

Before the two crucks joined at the roof apex, there was a cross-beam, usually a horizontal or tie beam. In wealthier areas, the farmers were able to employ trained carpenters rather than wood cutters to design an elaborate arch-brace with ornate designs – circles and cusps – carved in the beam. This was visible from floor level because no loft or storey existed and an elaborately carved arch-brace would be an attractive feature. Most of these carved beams are found in the wooded valleys of the eastern part of northern Wales – Clwyd, Dee, Alyn and Ceiriog. However, one strange example can be seen at Hafod Ysbyty in the remote mountain valley of Afon Gamallt near Ffestiniog. It is a 14th-15th Century house, originally in the form of a medieval hall-house, with the roof carried on a series of cruck couples the bases of which are lost in later stone walls. The apex of one of the crucks is carved into elaborate circles and cusps. There are no documentary records of owners or builders, but the house was built by a man of some wealth able to employ trained artisans rather than peasants. Hafod Ysbyty (summer hospice) may have been a refuge or sanctuary for travellers and pilgrims in days when no lodgings were available in these remote parts of Snowdonia. This may explain the legend, in Greek letters, 'Peace to this House' carved on a wooden lintel above the front door.

Ruthin. Cruck-framed house on Ruthin-Mold road.

15. BUILT BY A RACE OF GIANTS
HOUSES BUILT BETWEEN 1570-1620

Many houses from this period (1570-1620) survive because they were built of massive stones and incorporate 'new' features which gave comfort, warmth and privacy. There included glazed windows, internal wooden partitions, first-floor bedrooms and large fireplaces. They even included an internal lavatory or garderobe in exceptional cases. This Cyclopean style – named after the one-eyed giant, Cyclops – is found throughout north-eastern Wales and searching for examples is not difficult. Choose a valley wide enough for farming and with mountain grazing land, woods and rock outcrops, and there will still be a number of these Elizabethan – Jacobean houses standing and with relatively little change from their original structure. A good place to start is the Machno valley with a wealth of choices – Plas Glasgwm, Hafod Dwyryd, Coed-y-Ffynnon, Dugoed, Bennar – within three miles of Penmachno village. Documents with dates when they were built,

Dolwen. Main entrance to the house with cyclopean doorway.
Fine-grained granite building stone.

the original owners and constructional details are almost impossible to find, but much information can be inferred from their style and building methods. One legal document written in English on a sheep-skin parchment and dated 8th December, 1594, gives a precise record of a house at Llannerch-y-felin in the Conwy valley. The house was probably built about 1590, shortly before the Deed, which says that 'Huw ap Dafydd has given up and surrendered his right to Llannerch-y-felin, alias Tyddyn Lancaster, to Huw ap Owain (a relation, perhaps) and released his rights to the house but not the land'.

Llannerch-y-felin still survives, in excellent condition, in the village of Ro-wen. Its name, 'Glade of the Mill' suggests that there was a mill nearby so that the document and archaeology authenticates the date of the building in its present form with only one later addition. Houses like this were being built in the 1590's by yeoman farmers throughout northern Wales. Economic and social conditions were more settled and the wealthier farmers were anxious to build houses suited to their status. The main feature was a central doorway giving access to a cross-passage through the house from the front to the back. This passage, with fine oak partitions on each side, separated the hall – with its large fireplace and gable-end chimney – from the kitchen and buttery. The house at Llannerch-y-felin used the local materials which were strewn in abundance around the site. They were granite boulders deposited by glaciers and, later, by rivers from the mountains of Tal-y-fan and Drum. Large boulders were used for the foundations and lower courses and the corners where extra strength was needed. Some flat-edged stones were selected for the corners, but most of the rounded boulders project from thick layers of mortar. These boulders were not suitable for lintels over the doors and windows, so thick oak timbers were used and are still in place. The interior walls are also boulders, which are exposed and whitewashed, except in the best rooms where they are covered by oak partitions. There are beamed ceilings and massive timbers exposed over the fireplace. The finest internal features are the post and panel partition and the wooden staircase. In its day, Llannerch-y-felin would have stood out from the smaller houses of the village with their timber frames, mud walls and thatched roofs.

These sturdy houses with stone-mullion windows, an end-chimney and cross-passage were a feature of Elizabethan north-eastern Wales from Snowdonia towards the English Border, where they were replaced by half-timbered houses. Even in thickly wooded areas these 'cyclopean' stone houses can be found if there was a good outcrop of durable stone. A fine example is Dolwen near Llanarmon Dyffryn Ceiriog. With its river meadow, wooded slope, hill pasture and rock outcrops it epitomises the typical site for building about 1600. As at Llannerch-y-felin, huge blocks of granite were used for practically the whole of the building; only two small fields to the north of Dolwen the outcrop of green volcanic ash provided the building stone for the house. In 1928-30 this stone was quarried – Pentre Pant quarry – for the fine-grained granite suitable for making cubic blocks or setts used for paving town streets. Remains of the quarry are stanchions, a track down to the powder house on the river banks, piles of unused setts – 'the factory floor' – and the vertical quarry face above. It is unlikely that this hard stone was quarried in the 15th-16th centuries. Evidence from the broken-rock screes today suggest that there was then a plentiful supply of blocks and boulders which were ready-made for building. Many of these huge, unwrought boulders can be seen in the corner-walls and foundations of the house. For the door-jambs window frames and other walls the well-jointed granite was trimmed and dressed. After five centuries the weather has made no impact on this fine rock which is an attractive feature of the house. It is seldom that the building stone of a house can be traced without question to its original, geological source. Huge blocks of fine-grained granite were used for the door jambs and the main doorway is a 'cyclopean' structure of huge blocks roughly dressed, but with a fine keystone arch. A valuable clue to the dating of this style of building is shown by Galltfaen Isaf near Henllan, which has a Cyclopean door and a datestone inscriped '1601'. Inside Dolwen, oak timber was used for roof trusses, oak floor-boards, beams and the fine staircase; in 1600, dense oak forests still clothed the Ceiriog valley.

The cross-passage at Dolwen does not exist today, but ceiling

Llannerch-y-felin, Rowen.

timbers with holes and sockets are still intact and show where the partitions were and the doorways into the adjoining hall on one side with the kitchen – buttery on the other. In the kitchen, a small oak cupboard with an inscribed Tudor rose indicates a contemporary date. The fine oak staircase leads to the bedrooms with their thick unsupported ceiling beams and timber-framed walls with wattle and daub filling in the spaces between the exposed timbers. The ceiling beams are eighteen inches square and have carpenter's marks. One bedroom has an unusual feature – a lavatory or garderobe – which was a small room adjoining the chimney breast and projecting from the gable-end. A similar one can be seen at Plas Uchaf near Ruthin, where a walk-in entrance in the corner of the bedroom gives access to the garderobe, which does not project outside the wall; it is inserted into the side wall of the chimney. Garderobes were a feature of medieval castles and were essential in times of siege when waste could be discharged into the castle moat. Large numbers of them can be seen projecting from the walls of Conwy castle. However, the building of a garderobe at this time (circa 1600) was unusual and perhaps can be explained by the owner copying the idea from an older building elsewhere. At Bron-y-Foel in Llanenddwyn, a latrine block projects from the ground floor parlour and first floor chamber and discharges into a stream alongside the house. It is thought to be a copy of a similar block at the back of a 15th Century lodging at St Cross Hospital, Winchester. A master of St Cross once owned Bron-y-Foel and may have introduced this unique system of water sanitation to his remote part of Merioneth.

The garderobe at Dolwen is part of the west wing of the house, which has its own doorway – a low, narrow entrance with a wooden lintel – and all the features of a 'tower house' built for defence. The nearby Berwyn Mountains were a notorious refuge for lawless bandits until the mid-16th Century and this may have influenced the building plans for Dolwen. The west wing has a huge fireplace with a nine-foot long lintel, which is eighteen inches square. The end-wall chimney extends, tapering upwards, the height of four storeys and is similar to those found in medieval castles.

All of these 'new' features made for a great advance in comfort and privacy and, to judge by contemporary wills and inventories,

Massive stone blocks at Dolwen.

these houses would have been well furnished. In houses similar to Dolwen, the household goods would include feather beds, pillows, sheets, rough woollen coverings and, also in the bedrooms, a large cupboard, a chair and an old chest. Downstairs, the hall would have a large table, chairs and a high-backed settle side-on to the fireplace. On display there would be pewter jugs, dishes and cups. There would be brass candlesticks, a pewter salt-cellar and silver spoons. Knives were used, but it is unlikely that the Italian 'invention' – forks – would have found their way to Dolwen at this time. In the kitchen, there would be a lantern, stone troughs, churns, buckets, pans and dishes. There would be a large cauldron and a trivet. In the corner, there was an oak cupboard with the Tudor rose inscribed, which still survives.

Nothing evokes this period of building better and more intimately than the cross-passage – looking straight through the house from the entrance door to the garden at the back. The dark polished oak partitions of the passage adds to the attraction and the glimpse of the huge Tudor fireplace with burning logs. Some of the 'parish gentry', who lived in these houses, were Justices of the Peace and overseers of the church and parish affairs. They were conscious of their status and were proud to display a datestone or even a coat of arms on the stone lintel above the door.

Dolwen, Llanarmon Dyffryn Ceiriog.
The medieval-looking garderobe is set in
the angle between the front (west wing)
and the gable end chimney.

Dolwen.
Fine oak staircase.

16. THEATRE OF THE EMPIRE
OF GREAT BRITAIN
JOHN SPEED'S MAPS

Flint did not exist until the days of Edward I who, in 1277, marched into north-eastern Wales against the Welsh prince, Llywelyn. He decided that this site at Flint on the Dee estuary was perfect for a castle as the first step in the subjugation of Wales. The site was a low hill of sandstone projecting into the tidal waters of the Dee, which could get supplies by sea from Chester. Early letters suggest that it might have been named 'Le Caillon' (isolated rocks, in French) but 'Flynt' or 'Flint', which quickly gained acceptance, had the same meaning. As Edward took over the area known as 'Tegeingl' between the Dee estuary and the river Clwyd, he began, in the autumn of 1277, to build the castle and town of Flint. The policy of granting land to tenants (burgesses) from England and the setting up of a market was adopted from identical planned towns in English – occupied Aquitaine, where they were called 'bastides'. The town was laid out in a regular plan and was defended by a double bank with four entrance gates, which were closed at night. In three years, the castle was completed and the town was placed under the authority of the constable of the castle, who was also the mayor of the town. The previous two villages (vills) – Redington (mentioned in Domesday Book, 1086) and Ondeston – which had occupied the site – were swallowed up and the Welsh and Saxon villeins were dispersed. A church was built – St Mary's – and referred to for taxation purposes in 1291 as a 'chapel of Northop', with Master Benedict as the priest. The church survived until 1847 when, after years of neglect, it was demolished and medieval items such as silver pennies of Edward II, floor tiles, coffin lids and sepulchral slabs were found. There were four main streets running south-westwards from the castle and one street intersecting at the market square. This was the classic town plan of Edward's towns in Aquitaine and were intended to provide an economic and military base. The roll of names of the new burgesses were English or Norman-French incomers to Flint and some had

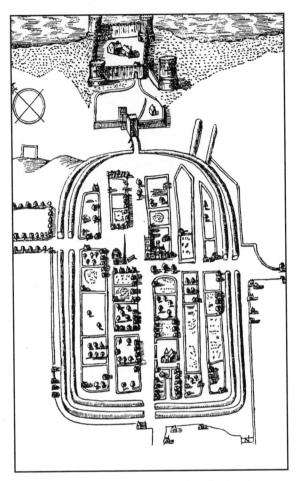

Flint castle and town, 1610, by John Speed.

their occupations listed. The castle was also based on a French model – in particular the castle design of Aigues Mortes on the Mediterranean coast near the Rhone delta. It had a round tower at each corner, curtain walls between them and one tower larger than the rest. This was a massive, thick-walled cylindrical tower, which formed a keep or donjon separated from the rest of the castle by a moat. It had immensely thick walls – over twenty-three feet – and was the last redoubt to which, in extreme peril, the garrison could

The Great Tower or Donjon of Flint castle.

escape. It was based on the mighty Tour de Constance in Aigues Mortes, which Edward had seen a few years earlier before embarking on a Crusade to recapture Jerusalem. This tower had only been completed a few years before his visit in 1266.

Flint was the first castle in Wales to be built by Edward I in this final campaign. The occupation of Wales was completed in 1284 with the Statute of Rhuddlan – Flint was given its full charter and borough status and was to be the blueprint of the castle-towns to be set up. Apart from the castle, which absorbed the finest building stone and had large bills for masons and carpenters, the biggest undertaking was the construction of ditches and ramparts around the town and a double bank projecting into the estuary. In this phase, nine hundred and fifty diggers were brought in from England. Even on early 20th Century maps, the sites of these medieval ditches were still clearly shown in the area where the town joined the castle and were still part of the landscape. From the 17th Century onwards there are references to 'Mount' as a mound, a field and finally 'Mount Street' which was a survival of this 13th Century rampart.

No map of Flint in 1284 was made, but a clear idea of the exact lay-out and details of banks, ditches and buildings can be seen in a map made in 1610 by John Speed. The town was then still in its medieval plan and was contained entirely within its original limits. It is also a good example of the cartographic skill of John Speed, who included it in an atlas called 'Theatre of the Empire of Great Britain', published in 1612. Speed was born in 1552, in Farndon, eight miles up the river Dee from Chester. He took up his father's trade as a tailor and in 1582 moved to London, married and became a Freeman of the Merchant Taylor Company. However, his interests were in drawing maps and investigating History at a time when both subjects were popular and creative. Christopher Saxton had been producing county maps of England and Wales; Camden and Norden were busy investigating History by visiting towns, houses, castles and making reports in their field-work. Speed was able to benefit from these resources and generously admitted that he 'put my sickle in other mens' corn'. His skills at map-making attracted a patron, Sir Fulke Greville, who obtained a post for him in Customs and, with Queen Elizabeth's support, he gained the freedom to travel widely and get to know the country. By 1612, under James I, who had united England with Scotland to make Great Britain, Speed recognized this in the title of his Atlas, 'The Theatre of the Empire of Great Britain'. Basing his maps on the earlier maps of Saxton and others, he produced maps of individual counties, including the thirteen counties of Wales. A major innovation was the addition of town maps, which were inserted in each county map. Of the seventy-three town plans in his Atlas, fifty were shown for the first time. These plans give detailed information about the lay-out of streets, some of which are named, and important buildings such as town halls, churches, castles, mills and even schools, where they existed. The accuracy of the map-work is remarkable, especially in the short time during which he travelled through 'every province in England and Wales'. Apart from the street plans and buildings, the maps showed details such as market crosses, maypoles, windmills, stocks and even gallows. All of this detail shows that the maps must have been the result of careful field survey. His methods are unknown, but like

Christopher Saxton, he probably sought out a few of the leading figures of the town from whom he extracted information. He then surveyed the town from a hill or tower to sketch its lay-out. He then measured distances to key points and used a 'scale of pases' (paces) to add authenticity and accuracy, which gives a modern feel to the map. The plan of the town had a 'bird's eye' perspective with buildings shown in side-elevation with larger buildings, such as castle and churches, being shown larger than houses. The idea of measuring the height of hills and mountains had not yet developed, so they are shown in side elevation as 'molehills' shaded on one side. Contour lines were unknown until 1730 and even then, were used only to show depth of water in river estuaries. Coastlines were shown in wavy lines to show the sea, which was confirmed by ships at sail and sea monsters. The maps were coloured and would have acted as an attractive and reliable traveller's guide, giving a pictorial record of towns mapped for the first time.

In his map of Flintshire (1610), Speed has an inset map of Flint, which was then the county town. It had not changed its lay-out since the 1280's and is therefore an uncanny record of the town and castle as it was in the days of Edward I. At the 'top' of the map – approximately north – the four towers of the castle are shown at the sea's edge with the large donjon standing on its own. The forecourt and gatehouse with the road into the town are exactly as laid out in 1280. The medieval walls and ditches are preserved intact with two banks projecting seawards. Four main streets are shown, including Church Street, shown by the position of the church. The lay-out of the houses and burgage plots still betray their medieval origins and the importance of pasture, crops and orchards within the town is shown.

It is at once an authentic plan of Flint in 1610, but also a valuable document of the town which Edward I established in 1284 and the first town to be built in northern Wales.

BEAUMARIS – SPEED'S MAP

John Speed's map of Beaumaris in 1611 is a superb record of the town as it was in his day. The broad stretch of marsh shows why

Edward I built his castle on this flat area – 'Beau marais' or 'fine marsh'. The two concentric rings of the castle are clearly shown and the moat – indicated by stippling – separating the castle from the town. The town walls and Watergate are clearly marked and even today small sections of the medieval wall still survive. In the early 19th Century, the town walls were washed by the sea at high tide. The main street from the castle led westwards to Watergate, which was a main entrance to the medieval town. By 1611, the town had expanded westwards outside the limits of the walls. At its intersection with Wexham Street, a town cross had once stood, but had disappeared by Speed's day. The church, with its large area of glebe land, and the market square, was a focal point and always busy. The streets were broad – even Clay Pit lane and Rotten Row – and the houses have generous burgage plots providing adequate food. The map also shows a Free School, the Friary on the hill at Llanfaes, a windmill and the important water-mill on the stream west of Britons Hill. The map is a fine representation of the town which – as the inset at the top of the map shows – was also a port at this time.

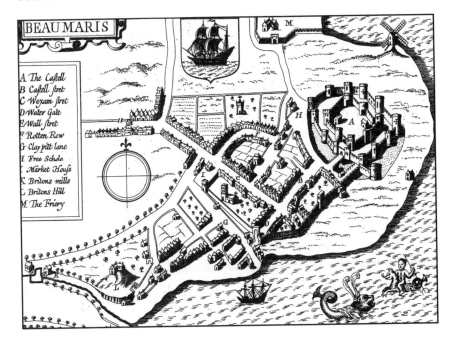

17. THE MAN WHO ASKED QUESTIONS
EDWARD LHUYD'S 'PAROCHIALIA'

Edward Lhuyd was born in Llanforden near Oswestry in 1660, and was educated at Oswestry Grammar School and Jesus College, Oxford which was noted for the number of Welsh students studying there. It was a period of great scientific and literary achievement, following the Restoration of Charles II in 1660; Wren, Newton and Pepys were working at this time and the Ashmolean Museum had just opened its doors in Oxford. From an early age, Edward Lhuyd had been interested in Botany and was drawn to the mountain plants of northern Wales. From a list of thirty-seven plants collected in the spring of 1682, he included one – the Snowdon Lily – which was later named after him, 'Lloydia Serotina'. This small bulb produces a few leaves and a purple-veined white flower, which grows on inaccessible ledges and has a short flowering season of two weeks in June. In Britain, it is only found in Snowdonia and, elsewhere in the world, is confined to Alpine or Arctic areas. It is thought to be a relic of plants which existed before the Ice Age, which it was miraculously able to survive in some parts of Snowdonia.

"Snowdon Lily"
– Lloydia Serotina.

To supplement his meagre resources whilst studying at Jesus College, he held two posts – as an assistant at the Ashmolean Museum and Register of Chemical Courses – which were awarded to students without much money. These posts encouraged his interest in Botany, Chemistry and Geology and enabled him to conduct field-work locally and also in Snowdonia. He travelled widely at a time when roads were bad and the earliest road-maps – such as those drawn by John Ogilby – were just being produced. Travel was on horse-back, but in Snowdonia there were no roads and very few horse

92

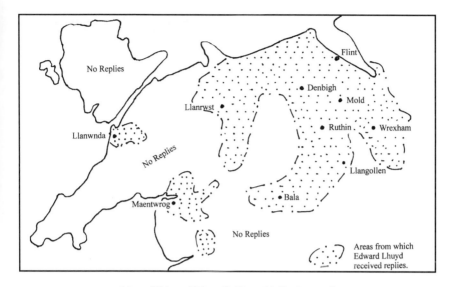

Map of Edward Lhuyd's 'Parochialia Queries'.

tracks. No one climbed mountains for pleasure and yet Lhuyd collected plants from Cader Idris, the Arans near Bala and in Snowdonia, where he specialized in high-altitude plants such as club mosses, saxifrages and mountain sorrel.

In 1691, at the age of 31, Lhuyd was appointed keeper of the Ashmolean Museum and continued his field visits to collect specimens, which now included fossils, particularly fossil-plants from the Coal Measures of Denbighshire. His drawings of these fossils excited great interest because, at this time, Geology did not exist as a scientific study and no one knew how fossils had originated. Lhuyd formed a small Geology club and trained students to collect and record fossils and got money to support their travelling and living costs; this was the beginning of the study of Palaeontology, with a catalogue of fossils collected and shown at the Ashmolean Museum.

In 1695, he began to extend his interest into History and Archaeology and aimed at compiling a record of these aspects – as well as Natural History – in Wales, using undergraduates to distribute a set of questions to each parish in Wales. About four thousand of these 'parochial queries' were distributed to the

93

gentry, clergy and schoolmasters; he personally travelled on foot with three friends 'to pry into every hole and corner', which became 'a tedious ramble'. He compiled notebooks, with information about villages, towns, forts, monasteries, bridges, coins and all aspects of History such as Roman remains and even prehistoric monuments. He received a detailed letter with a plan of the motte and bailey castle at Tomen y Rhodwydd near Llandegla and gave a full account of the Chambered Tomb at Capel Garmon. He received answers – some in English, others in Welsh – from the parishes which had accepted his questions. The best response came from Flintshire – where practically all the parishes responded – and the old county of Denbighshire. A large batch of replies came from the eastern half of Merioneth, with all the parishes around Bala Lake keen to respond to his queries. As a result, his book 'Parochialia' was published in 1698, and it is an excellent source book for the final years of the 17th Century in north-eastern Wales.

A good example of his work is the recording of the names and locations of bridges, which were becoming important as road transport improved. At this time, John Ogilby, the chief cartographer of Charles II, was producing road-maps which showed bridges for the first time. Many bridges had been built in northern Wales in the 17th Century and those mentioned in 'Parochialia' can be readily identified by name with their exact locations. In the parish of Llanfor near Bala he records five bridges:

1. Pont y Bala on the river Tryweryn just 'over the lower end of Bala'.
2. Pont Rhywaedog 'opposite the church one mile off'.
2a. Pont y Keynant 'a quarter of a mile below'.
3. Pont Rhyd Ffraink 'on the Meloch below the church'.
4. Pont Meloch 'a quarter of a mile below where Meloch falls to the Dee'.

These can be accurately pinpointed and some have not been rebuilt since 1698, particularly on minor roads. Pont y Keynant – now more accurately called 'Pont y Ceunant' (the Bridge over the Ravine) – is still standing as it crosses the narrow gorge on the old road from Bala to Llangurig. Here, the river Hirnant has cut a deep narrow gorge and was spanned by a single-arched bridge.

In the neighbouring parish of Llanycil, which extends northwards from Bala lake to the wild moorland of the Migneint, nine bridges are recorded, each one identified by name and position. One of the bridges is referred to in an ingenious manner in the remote Migneint, where there are no striking landmarks:

PONT RHYD Y PORTHNYN YM MIKNIT TY HWNT I'R TAI HIRION YNG HYLCH TERVYNE YSBYTY TRAWSFYNYDD A PHESTINIOG.

This can be translated as:

THE BRIDGE OF THE DROVERS' CROSSING IN MIGNEINT BEYOND THE LONG HOUSES AT THE BOUNDARY OF YSBYTY (IFAN) TRAWSFYNYDD AND FFESTINIOG.

Edward Lhuyd was anxious to locate bridges by giving a reference to their position relative to a town, village, church or mill and its distance from these fixed points. The Migneint had no such places; it was an ill-defined area of moorland waste, straddling the headwaters of four major river systems – the Prysor, Cynfal, Serw and Tryweryn rivers. It is a featureless tract of peat-bog and rough grass and without trees lying between Ysbyty Ifan, Trawsfynydd and Ffestiniog. It was an important crossing area for Drovers moving their cattle towards Bala and the English Border. Here in Migneint, cattle could be moved fairly easily with ample room for large herds and pasture as they moved cattle from Llŷn and the tidal salt marshes of the Dwyryd estuary up the Prysor valley from Trawsfynydd or the Vale of Ffestiniog and converged on this important crossing, which is appropriately named PONT RHYD Y PORTHMYN (Bridge of the Drovers' Crossing). It was described as being just beyond Tai Hirion, which survived as a roofless ruin until 1980. The bridge still survives and is a remarkable example of a local 17th Century bridge built of drystone, trimmed blocks with a keystone arch with no parapet or kerb. Later – when the Drovers ceased using it – it became a relic, because it was too narrow for the 18th Century coaches which rattled their way across the moors from Bala to Ffestiniog. It is fortunate that it has survived and that it was recorded by Lhuyd.

18. THE WHITE GATES WERE NEVER OPENED

Much of the Georgian landscape in the Alyn valley around Mold is still intact – the gracious houses are set amidst parkland and river meadows, which recall the early 18th Century. Old families, such as the Wynnes and the Eytons lived comfortable lives in their elegant Georgian houses set well back from the main Mold to Wrexham Road. The Wynnes were living in Leeswood Old Hall and John Wynne, in 1695, married the daughter of Humphrey Jones, who lived in the nearby lead-rich Halkyn Mountain. John Wynne left his lands to his eldest son George, and in 1715, lead was discovered; the mine became one of the richest in Halkyn, yielding £340,000 in 20 years and, eventually, a million pounds by 1735. This unprecedented wealth enabled George to move out of the impoverished minor-gentry class; so he built, for £40,000, a splendid new house on land adjoining Leeswood Old Hall. To the annoyance of his Tory neighbours, the Eytons, he became a Whig M.P. His status was still further enhanced when, in 1731, he bought a baronetcy. A portrait of George Wynne, painted in 1727 when he was only 27, by Vanderbank, shows him with a blue velvet coat, white satin vest and a gold-topped cane, looking the part of an aspiring 18th Century squire. The new Leeswood Hall was built as a three-storey Palladian house with a recessed centre and two extensive wings in a striking hill-top position with landscaped gardens with parkland, groves and a yew-walk. The entrance to this large estate was guarded by two lodges built of brown limestone in classical style with pediments and adjoining Black Gates.

Fortunately, George Wynne also decided to build the remarkable 'White Gates', which lie on a quiet country lane west of the Mold-Wrexham road. He was determined to build something to show his wealth and probably chose gates because they were the most obvious and fashionable status symbol at this time. Some years earlier, a French Huguenot, Jean Tijou, had introduced wrought-iron designs for screens to be executed in churches and fine houses, but also outside as entrances to their estates and sometimes flanked by gate-houses. Jean Tijou worked in

The White Gates of Leeswood Hall.

Chatsworth, Hampton Court (for the royal family) and in Wren's St Paul's Cathedral. He left pattern books, which were bought by wealthy families such as the Myddletons of Chirk castle and so these pattern-books were passed on by these wealthy patrons to local blacksmiths. One of the most famous blacksmiths in northern Wales was Robert Davies, who had a smithy, inherited from his father, at Croes Foel near Bersham. He could get any thickness of bar iron and sheet iron from the nearby Bersham furnace where, in 1715, iron was being smelted by using the vast local charcoal resources. Davies was commissioned to build the Chirk castle gates in 1711-12, getting iron bars from the Pont-y-Blew forge near Chirk and he took over the smithy at Chirk castle itself. The gates were not completed until 1719 because two of the Myddletons died in this period and Robert Davies was uncertain of the completion of the commission. The making of these gates was a massive undertaking; each detailed feature of the gates was the work of a smith for days. Davies worked on other commissions and wagon loads of iron from Bersham furnace were a feature of transport on the badly-surfaced roads around Wrexham. The clerk at the furnace – John Kelsall, who was appointed in 1720 – kept a day-to-day diary and records the visits of Davies to Bersham to buy iron and settle accounts. On 13th May, 1726, Kelsall records a visit to

Wynne at Leeswood 'went to see the Collier's at Pontblyddyn . . . Then went to the Wynnes of the Tower (Mold). I viewed some cordwood and bid him 10s 6d per cord (128 cu.feet) but could not agree'. Cordwood had a specified diameter and length suitable for making charcoal.

This period was of great importance in the making of iron using charcoal to fuel the furnaces; the revolutionary substitution of coal for coking the furnaces was just beginning. This was the greatest period for wrought-iron working in Britain and it was not unusual for George Wynne to decide to use his fortune to build gates. There are no documents to prove categorically that Robert Davies was given the commission but, as stated, John Kelsall visited Wynne as a customer for cordwood. Robert Davies was busy making gates for Wrexham and Ruthin churches as well as the chancel screen for Mold Church and he was at the height of his powers in the 1720's.

George Wynne, thanks to the money from the Halkyn lead-mine, could compete with the Myddletons and bid for the best workmanship in hand-made wrought iron, and afford the best quality iron made in Bersham. The 'White Gates' are a massive one hundred feet long, consisting of gates and an ornamental screen supported by masonry piers at each end. They are, in effect, a screen which is one of the finest and most remarkable in Britain. They were never intended to be used as working gates or for passage of vehicles as is shown on old engravings, which do not show an approach road or drive. Built in 1726, at the height of the lead mining boom, they were placed at the foot of the hill on which the Hall stood in its Palladian splendour. They were intended to embellish the view of the Hall from the west and have outlasted the original house itself. After George Wynne's daughter died in 1798, the Hall was bought by the Rev. Wynne-Eyton, who reduced the hall dramatically by removing the top storey and the two wings. A descendant, Mrs Wynne-Eyton died in 1981 and the Gates came under the control of the 'White Gates Charitable Fund' which restored and repainted them in 1985 for £12,000.

There were many notable smiths at work in England and Wales in the 1720's who were disciples, but not pupils, of Jean Tijou and using his design books. Without actual records, accounts and

White Gates at Leeswood Hall (seen in the background).
Dolphin (cypher of Sir George Wynne at the apex of the gate).

Leeswood Old Hall – home of George Wynne. Now considerably reduced in size.

invoices, it is difficult to name the blacksmith involved in making the White and Black Gates. Circumstantial evidence and the similarities with wrought iron work at Eaton Hall, Chirk castle and the entrances to Ruthin and Wrexham churchyards, suggest that the Leeswood work was done by Robert Davies of Croes Foel. His red-brick Georgian house, with its identifying blue plaque, still stands near Bersham and, in later years, he became a yeoman farmer. In building the Black Gates, he used a simpler style and they were placed on either side of two gate-houses and were used as the entrance to the Hall from the Mold Road. Recently, they were removed and placed at the entrance drive to the Tower. The original crest on the top of the gates was the Wynne dolphin; later this was replaced by the Eyton family lion rampant, but G.W. (George Wynne) forms the cipher beneath it. Apart from a leaf scroll, which was damaged and replaced later, the rust-free condition of the gates is attributed to the charcoal-smelted iron used in their original construction from the Bersham furnace in the 1720's. The Tower also houses the famous Vanderbank portrait of Sir George Wynne and keeps his memory alive.

It is fortunate that Sir George Wynne had the money and insight to build the screen and gates at the time when design and wrought-ironwork were at their best. Shortly afterwards, in 1730-40, cast iron replaced wrought iron because it was cheaper. The same structural and decorative work could be done by casting instead of costly and laborious work by hand. Also, ideas about landscape, introduced by 'Capability Brown', stressed an open landscape dotted with trees forming a parkland with extensive vistas unimpeded by gates and screens. A feature of the 'new' landscape was the 'ha-ha' – a sunken fence bounding a park or garden.

Sir George Wynne,
Leeswood Hall – portrait
now in Tower, Mold.

Sir George Wynne left a remarkable legacy but, unfortunately, squandered his fortune and died in 1756, in debt, at Blackheath.

19. THE LEGAL-TENTH
TITHE BARNS

In England during the Middle Ages the people in the manorial villages gave a tenth of their income – in the form of goods – known as 'the legal tenth' or tithe to provide a living for the parish priest. As the parish system spread to Wales during the 12th and 13th Centuries, this tithe was collected as 'degwm' or 'tithe'. This applied equally to corn, lambs, milk, eggs and milk produced during the year and detailed records of these tithes survive in the parish registers. An account of the vicar of Bodfari's income in the reign of Henry VIII for the year 1535 gives these details in shillings (5p) and pence:

	£	s	d
Goat's milk and wool		3	4
Lambs		4	8
Cow's milk		3	8
Flax, hemp, fruit, chickens		4	0
Grain and hay	6	0	0

Photograph of the Tithe Barn in Glynceiriog in the 1930's
(now a house – Ysgubor Ddegwm).

The main income collected by the vicar was from corn and hay, which were given at one particular time of the year – late summer, at harvest time. It was, therefore, necessary to store the corn and hay for use during the winter months so that tithe barns were built either near the church or the rectory where the vicar himself had glebe land. There is nothing special to distinguish them from ordinary barns so that a typical building for corn storage would have two large doors on opposite walls, so that a strong draught could help the process of winnowing – separating the chaff from the grain on the barn floor. The threshed grain was then stored in bays on either side of the doors and put into sacks ready to be taken to the mill to be made into flour. Whilst the grain was in storage, ventilation was essential to prevent mould and overheating. The sides of the barn were marked by a series of narrow slits to allow air to filter into the barn. On the interior walls, holes in the masonry were left for barn owls to perch and watchfully prevent mice and rats from consuming the vital grain. Sometimes, these tithe barns were later extended into farm-houses, but can still be identified by the original ventilation slits. A fine example is at Llanfynydd, where the farm itself has taken the name 'Tithe Barn', and is shown as such on the O.S. map. It was probably the upland storage for hay for the large lowland parish of Hope, some distance away, and with its own tithe barn surviving until recently, near the church. When Llanfynydd became a parish itself in 1846, the role of hay collection for tithe purposes was redundant, so it became part of the farm itself, which retained the old name.

Often, the best surviving evidence is the retention of the name 'tithe barn' or 'ysgubor ddegwm'. These names are attached to many cottages across northern Wales, from the remotest corner of Llŷn Peninsula to the Dee estuary. The small roadside cottage 'Ysgubor Ddegwm', near Bodfari, still retains the first-floor doorway in the gable-end through which the hay was hoisted to the loft. In other cottages, the narrow ventilation slits have been retained in the thick outer walls.

One of the finest unaltered tithe barns in north-eastern Wales, dating back to the early years of the 16th Century, lies on a rock ledge overlooking the farmhouse at Plas Iolyn. It is built of large unhewn boulders with square corner stones and attached to a three-storeyed pele tower which was the original 'castle' of the local war-lord at an earlier period. At first sight, Plas Iolyn looks an unlikely spot for a tithe-barn, since it is over three miles from the nearest church at Ysbyty Ifan – an area notorious for bandits until the early 16th Century. This remote upland area was used mainly for pasture and was part of the sheep-rearing grange of Aberconwy Abbey – Tir yr Abad (The Abbot's Land). The local war-lord at this time, and who built the house at Plas Iolyn, was Rhys ap Meredydd also known as Sir Rhys ap Meredydd of Hiraethog, who comes into the record as the leader of a band of fighters at the Battle of Bosworth. He had borne the standard of the future Henry VII and after Bosworth, was rewarded with honours and land in this area. His son – Sir Robert ap Rhys – also benefited and became chaplain and cross-bearer of Cardinal Wolsey, the chief minister of the next king – Henry VIII.

The 12 foot square pele tower at Plas Iolyn is the main surviving remains of the old house. The long narrow tithe barn was tied in to the upper storey of this older tower, probably by Sir Robert ap Rhys.

These buildings were then inherited by Sir Robert's son, Dr Ellis Price, who was educated in Cambridge University and gained a Doctorate in Law. When Henry VIII dissolved the monasteries (1536), he appointed Ellis Price as one of his Commissioners to dispose of Tir yr Abad and later, in 1560, Ellis Price obtained half of this land as well as rectories at Llandrillo-yn-Rhos and Llanuwchllyn. At this time in the reign of Elizabeth, he attained great power in northern Wales through his association with the Earl of Leicester, one of Elizabeth's favourites. Ellis Price gained additional rectories at Denbigh and Llaniestyn and substantial tithes. This accounts for the use of the long, narrow barn which is still known as 'The Tithe Barn'. As he got wealthier from the additional tithes, he found it necessary to build another barn in the courtyard, opposite the earlier one. Here, he had a carpenter inscribe the date 1572 in the lettering style of the time on one of the horizontal beams in the barn. This still survives and reminds us of the corruption, oppression of the tenants and lavish life-style of

Tithe Barn with name plate Ysgubor Degwm at Llangian, Llŷn.
Note – ventilation slits also on the gable end.

Ellis Price at the end of the 16th Century.

Tithe Barns deserve more attention before their history is completely lost. Many have been demolished, but some have been adapted or rebuilt as houses. Often the only evidence is the retention of the name 'ysgubor ddegwm', but there is sometimes a clue in the structure of the building to show its former history. In Llangian in Llŷn, there is a small tithe barn which still retains its Welsh name but, even though it has been rebuilt as a house, it has kept the narrow ventilation slits in the main walls facing the road. The local church dates to the late 13th Century – with the original rubble boulders still visible in the footings – but the tithe barn was probably built in the 15th Century when the church was rebuilt and extended.

Similarly in Glyn Ceiriog, the village tithe barn survives as a modern house, but with its old name. It lies near what was the original centre of the village, opposite the Rectory, before the village expanded southwards as a result of slate quarrying and the

Glyn Valley Tramway. The barn was still in its original condition until the 1970's, with the gable-ends and groundfloor built of coursed rubble with large boulder footings. One gable-end had a hay-loft door and there was a wide door at the main street entrance. The lower gable-end is still coarse masonry and a large rectangular block has survived and is thought to have been a horse-mounting block for visitors to the Rectory. The tithe barn is not situated near the hillside church, because the road was too steep for horse-drawn carts.

A few miles down the valley from Glynceiriog, at Llwyn-mawr, a valuable diary records how, in 1816, a fourteen-year old boy, John Hughes, helped his uncle to collect tithes for Sir Watkin Williams Wynne – from one side of the valley above Llwyn-mawr. They used a horse and cart and, on the steeper slopes, a sledge for carrying corn to the tithe barn at Llwyn-mawr. The diary records the names of the farms – Brithdir, Tal-y-garth, Cae Mor, Penllwyn and Llangwryd – which were connected by a network of narrow lanes to the Tithe Barn at Llwyn-mawr. The barn had two cowsheds with an attached acre of land for grazing bullocks. In winter, John Hughes had the job of chopping up straw and turnips for making a mash for winter fodder for the cattle. After the Commutation Act of 1836, money payment was substituted for payment in goods so that Tithe Barns became redundant. In this case, John Hughes' brother bought the Tithe Barn and converted it into stone cottages, which still survive but give no clue about their history.

20. DATES TO REMEMBER
DATE INSCRIPTIONS

Dates are the 'stuff' of History; dates inscribed on stone or carved in wood, provided they are in situ and have not been re-used, give an exact date of the age of the building. Date-inscriptions are important archaeological evidence especially where there are no documents and they begin at the time when the first storeyed houses were being built in north-eastern Wales. The large number of Elizabethan inscriptions in Flintshire and Denbighshire and Wrexham is due to the large numbers of educated minor gentry, who were anxious to express their status in wealth and learning.

The earliest date-inscription is at Plas Uchaf, an Elizabethan manor house near Llangollen, where the lettering above the south-west door reads:

MDLVIII

ELIZABETH REGINA

Plas Uchaf.
World's End, Llangollen.

which gives 1563 as the date of building. However, this date-stone is not authenticated, although the architectural style of solid masonry blocks at the base with herring-bone half timbering above and the 'tooth-topped' chimneys, indicates an early Elizabethan building. In north-eastern Wales, date plaques started in the 1560's and became fashionable from 1570 onwards. The period when they are most commonly found on the houses of the gentry and well-to-do farmers was 1650-1720 and often coincided with periods when farming was prosperous and a date-inscription was considered to be a mark of wealth and social status. The

Date inscribed on beam in barn at
Plas Iolyn near Pentrefoelas.

commonest places for the inscriptions were just below the eaves or above the door at the front of the house.

Of equal importance are the dates of this period (late-16th century) carved in wood on the interior of buildings and which have been perfectly preserved. Plas Iolyn, near Pentrefoelas, was built in the reign of Henry VIII by Robert Price, who was chaplain to Henry's Chancellor – Cardinal Wolsey. The house drew valuable tithes from Price's church livings and an old tithe barn, still surviving, was used to store grain. His son, Dr Ellis Price, inherited the house and also acquired more tithes which necessitated the building of a new tithe-barn, which still has its date inscribed on an interior beam. The date – 1572 – is in bas-relief (raised lettering) on the collar of a roof-truss and enclosed in a separate panel at the lower edge of the beam. The letter 'I' is tailed and ringed and the '5' and '7' are flat-topped. It is an authentic date because of its similarity to the so-called 'Rhiwlas Lettering', whereby the letters are distinctive with the '5's' drawn in the Elizabethan manner without squared corners. A similar dated beam can be seen in a barn at Gellilyfdy in Flintshire (1586) and in the old house of Rhiwlas (1574), now demolished, near Bala where another member of the Price family lived. Rhiwlas was built in 1574 as shown by the date inscribed in the main partition screen; it reads:

THE GRACE OF GOD BE IN THYS HOUSE
ANNO DOMINI: 1574

and, although the house was demolished (in 1955), the screen and inscription were preserved and a new house built. Nine years later, a similar house was built at Plas Newydd, Cefn which had an inscription (1583), which was made by the same carpenter who worked at Rhiwlas. These inscriptions were the work of an unknown carpenter, who has left at least fifteen of these wood-inscribed panels from Bala to Prestatyn and falling within the period 1570 to 1598. He worked mainly in the houses of the closely-knit families in the north-eastern corner of Wales. Some of the inscriptions were commissioned by the church with a very fine carved panel displayed in the medieval church of Caerhun in the Conwy valley.

The placing of date-stones on the front walls – usually above the door – of houses became common in the 17th Century and were even placed on ordinary farmhouses, such as the long houses – Tai Hirion – on the wild moors of the Migneint. This is referred to in George Borrow's 'Wild Wales' when he was crossing the Migneint from Ffestiniog to Bala in 1862. He saw 'a range of white buildings, diverging from the road on the right hand, the gable of the first abutting upon it with a kind of farm-yard before them. A respectable-looking woman was standing in the yard. I went up to her and inquired the name of the place. These houses, sir, she said are called Tai Hirion, Migneint – look over the door and you will see T.H.; which letters stand for Tai Hirion. Migneint is the name of the place where they stand. I looked and upon a stone which formed the lintel of the middle most door I read T.H. 1630. The words Tai Hirion, it will be as well to say, signify the long houses. I looked long and steadfastly at the inscription, my mind full of thoughts of the past'.

Tai Hirion was mainly a sheep farm, with some cattle, in one of the remotest parts of the great moorland plateau of the Migneint. It was mentioned as a house by name in Edward Lhuyd's 'Parochialia' in 1698 and remained occupied by a shepherd and his family until the 1940's. It was abandoned shortly afterwards, when a cattle grid across the road made the shepherd's job unnecessary. It is now only a pile of stones by the roadside and the nearby stream, Afon Tai Hirion, is its only legacy. No trace of the lintel date-stone exists although it may have survived as a re-used stone for building roadside walls, or even the bridge near the important cattle grid. A T.V. programme, made about 1972 by John Seymour,

Chweleiriog Goch near Llandegla.
Date-inscription above first-floor window.

following in George Borrow's footsteps, showed the old house with the lintel date-stone still intact.

Sometimes, a date-inscription gives a vital clue to changes in building style or even the use of new building materials. An interesting and curious case is the fine brick house of Chweleiriog Goch near Llandegla. Including the cellar and an attic, it is an imposing house made of brick in an area with thick limestone beds and where all the old houses are built of local limestone. Due to the poor road surfaces, in the days before the Turnpike Trusts had been set up, overland transport of heavy, bulky goods, such as bricks, was slow and costly. The nearest source of bricks was at Brymbo, which was six miles away across the Llandegla moors. At this time – the 1730's – a cart-load of coal or lime over that distance, cost an exhorbitant three pounds.

The house at Chweleiriog Goch was built on a foundation of limestone, which can still be seen under the brickwork and it appears in the spiral staircase of worn steps down to the cellar. However, the cellar itself has a fine vaulted roof of mortared brick similar to a cellar in an old house, Mount Pleasant, in Brymbo. The three storeys are made of bricks with two corbels at the front at first and second floor levels. These corbels are projections of two layers of brickwork separated by a normal course of bricks. The lower corbel corresponds with the first-floor level and the second with the high attic floor. A date-stone lies above the upper corbel and just below roof level. The date-stone which can be seen from the farm-yard reads:

I

E   M

1739

and is set in a neat stone insert in the brick facade. The top letter refers to the surname and the lower letters to the husband and wife; perhaps they were newly married and setting up home in 1739.

The use of brick, emphasized by the word 'Goch' (red), at this time is puzzling, but the datestone is authentic. A plausible theory is that there may be a connection with the nearby Elizabethan mansion of Bodidris on the large Mostyn Estate. By the first decade of the 18th Century, improved living conditions were bringing changes, even to remote areas such as the bleak Llandegla moors. The small farms were mainly straw-thatched limestone buildings but in the accounts of Bodidris there are bills for 1704-6 to show that cart-loads of bricks, probably from Brymbo, and slates were being brought in across the moors. No record of bills exist to reveal details of the building materials used at Chweleiriog Goch but, at least, there is evidence that these 'new' materials, bricks and slates, were now available here. A few years later the farmer placed an identical date-stone on a barn across the farmyard at Chweleiriog Goch which reads:

I

I   A

1764

which shows continued confidence in the use of bricks.

Some houses evolve and it is important to examine the exact placing of the datestone; a good example is the lovely white-washed house of Hafod Dwyryd overlooking a terraced lawn, trees and a mountain stream near Penmachno. Originally built in the late 16th Century, it was a small square house of thick rubble walls, large corner stones of local slate and small roofing slates. It was extended sidewards into a rectangular house in 1600 with windows; chimneys were built into the side walls. The house was built by the Anwyl family, who were descended from Gruffudd ap Cynan (d.1137), a powerful ruler of Gwynedd. The ruins of their medieval house stands above its 16th Century replacement on the hillside at Parc near Llanfrothen and near the sea and the beautiful Dwyryd estuary, after which the 'new' house of Hafod Dwyryd was named as a reminder of their homeland. By 1678, they had become wealthy enough to display their gentry status by building a fine two-storeyed slate porch, inscribed R.A. 1678, for Richard Anwyl – above the wide arched doorway and which only identifies the date of the porch.

It is always satisfying to see a well-preserved date-stone on a house which itself is in good condition and with little external change since the time it was built. This gives an instant record and such date-stones are undemanding of the local historian's time; there is no need to search for old documents or maps because the evidence is at once clear and unequivocal. The date-stone (1746) above the door of a roadside cottage at Llanfwrog near Ruthin, with its typical gable-end to the road, shows with exact precision the scale, dimensions and architectural style of an ordinary village house of the Georgian period in the Vale of Clwyd.

Brynffynnon – cottage in Llanfwrog. Datestone (1746) also shows owners:

I

H   E

21. THE POST-HORN DISTURBS THE PEACE AT 3 A.M.
PLYMOUTH HOUSE, NORTHOP

There is a long tradition of building in stone in Northop – the church itself, the old school in the churchyard, the smithy and the old cottages in the High Street. A search for the 'parish rock' takes us along the loose gravel of Quarry Lane to one of the main sources of the biscuit – and honey – coloured sandstone. Quarry Farm, west of Northop, stands on these massive beds which could be prised from the outcrop by wedges and hammers into building stone. From Tudor times, the best quality stone was reserved for the church, which was enlarged by the addition of another nave and the magnificent tower, which was started in the reign of Henry VII and only completed in the reign of his granddaughter, Elizabeth. Heraldic devices – a portcullis, a fleur de lys, three lions and a Tudor rose – above the Tudor doorway, give clues as to its date. The magnificent Late Perpendicular Tower compares with those of contemporary churches at Wrexham (one of the 'Seven Wonders of Wales'), Gresford and Mold and suggests the importance of Northop at this time. It is out of proportion to the village and is reminiscent of the great 'wool churches' of the Cotswolds. Another important building at that time – in the High Street – was referred to as 'Tŷ Mawr' (the Big House). Today the main house in the High Street is Plymouth House, which is incongruously built in red bricks, but on a foundation of sandstone. This is best seen in the mullion windows, which are vertical stone shafts (window frames) of the basement. In Tudor times, this was the ground floor, but is now the cellar with a stone flagged floor, huge oak beams, a low ceiling and a brick-lined well in the floor. It is likely that this house (Tŷ Mawr, perhaps) was built in 1530 and is therefore contemporary with the new building work then being carried out in the church. The house became part of the Earl of Bridgewater's Estate when he inherited the Manor of Northop in 1605, so it was the Manor House and Court House, where affairs of the manor were settled. At this time, also, Northop

Plymouth House, Northop. Wide coach entrance gate and stables behind the house.

(in 1602) became officially a 'Post Town' on the Post Road from London via Chester to Holyhead. Since the time of Henry VIII, news and intelligence to and from Ireland was carried by post-boys riding horseback as a courier in the service of Henry VIII and, later, Elizabeth. Each town on the route – Northop, Denbigh, Conwy, Beaumaris and Holyhead – had to provide accommodation, stables for changing horses and fresh horses, and, by the end of the 17th Century, this eventually led to the growth of coaching inns.

By 1670, the manor house was sold to Roger Whitley and was demolished to the ground floor where the mullion windows at the front still survive, and the foundations of this older house (1530) are still fully exposed. In 1672-3, Roger Whitley built a new house using brick on these foundations; it had four sets of windows at the front, four chimney stacks and its four storeys made it the 'Big House' of the village. It had a front balcony facing the High Street and a window overlooking a fine cobbled courtyard and, although bricked up later, the door can still be seen on the third floor.

Roger Whitley had been a Colonel in the Royalist Army of Charles I and returned to the area after Charles II's Restoration (1660) to buy and rebuild the old manor house at Northop. Internally, the most striking feature is the oak staircase, which has finely-carved banisters and ornate newel posts. It is exactly like staircases put up in nearby houses – at Walgoch and Rhual – which have been dated to 1628-40, and it is thought that the staircase is in situ and was part of the old house. The carved banisters stop on the first floor where the main bedrooms are, and a plainer style continues to the servants' quarters on the upper floor. The massive oak-beamed ceilings in the bedrooms and the thick oak-plank floors are also a fine feature and indicate a high level of building and wealth. In the servants' bedrooms some savings were made by using untrimmed bark of raw oak. There is also evidence of the use of ships' timbers, especially above a fireplace in one bedroom; a plank with a narrow, horizontal groove held a ship's rope and pulley. Other timbers may have had the same source, which is not surprising with Northop's position, which is only two miles from the then-navigable river Dee. Sir Roger Whitley became an M.P. for Chester and Mayor of Chester so that the new house befitted his wealth and status. He had a portrait painted; a memorial plaque to him survives in Hawarden church and he was buried in 1697, in Hawarden.

The Earl of Plymouth, who had married Whitley's daughter, inherited the house and a 1717 map shows the house as the largest in the village with land running to Northop Brook. Shortly afterwards – with Northop's growing importance on the improved roads – it was adapted as a coaching inn named 'The Yacht'. Wide entrance gates, room for coaches, stables, a smithy and adaptations in the house made it into the premier coaching inn in Northop. By 1776, it was one of a 'chain' of coaching inns on the main road from Chester to Holyhead. Northop was the first stop out of Chester for stage-coaches where horses could be changed. The barn at the back of the house was made into stables which had room for twelve horses; one block had six horse troughs and a sleeping area for the coachman, with a small fireplace linked to the main chimney of the house. Next to this block was an arched doorway and place for a coach and another six horse troughs and a swilling area. The inn always had six fresh horses for the onward journey and six places for those horses which had completed the strenuous eleven mile uphill run from Chester to this convenient overnight stop. An old

Plymouth House (Northop). Original stone house with mullion windows forms foundations of 'new' brick house. This is now the cellar with a well.

milestone near the inn still survives and shows the distance of eleven miles to Chester. The Royal Mail left Chester and rumbled through Northop at 8.30 a.m. on its way to Holyhead. The return coach with the clatter of hooves and the sounding of the post-horn disturbed the residents of High Street in the village at 3 a.m. There were other inns in Northop, eight altogether, but the 'Yacht' was the main coaching inn with plenty of room for coaches, horses and people. In 1776, it was acquired by Thomas Carter as one of a chain of inns or post-houses which provided a high standard of accommodation. In May 16 1776, he announced a special service for the nobility and gentry between Chester and Holyhead. 'I am induced to establish a line of post houses between Chester and Holyhead where the public may be accommodated with carriages and horses at the same rates as on English roads. A Stage Coach will set out from the Yacht Inn, Chester and from the Wash's Head,

Holyhead, on Monday, July 22 and every following morning at 4 o'clock and arrive at each place the same evening – to carry 3 passengers only at £1.11.6d each, to be allowed 10lb luggage. Performed by the following innkeepers, who have provided neat fast coaches, post chaises, horses etc:

Thomas Carter, Yacht Inn, Chester
Thomas Bellis, Yacht Inn, Northop
Robert Morris, White Lion, St Asaph
W. Oakes, King's Head, Conwy
Thomas Carter, Bangor Ferry
Sam Watkin, Wash's Head, Holyhead

At this time, the Yacht in Northop, like other coaching inns, was equal to the demand of one or more overnight coaches. Large bedrooms with open fireplaces and beds with flock or feather mattresses were standard. Plumbing and piped water were unknown, but there was a source of fresh water from the spring-fed well in the cellar. The hooks and nails in the thick beams was where the beef, mutton and game were hung before being cooked and taken to the parlour. Here, the food was served on a large common table. Ale brewed by the innkeeper was preferred to water. The parlour was also the centre of news and gossip and, no doubt, the hazards of travelling by stage-coach. With the continued improvement of Turnpike Trust roads, Northop became a central point in the road system with three toll-gates operating in the village.

This was the golden age for the Yacht; gradually, from 1810, Northop declined, year by year, as a coaching centre. In 1808, the London to Holyhead route was opened up from Shrewsbury through Betws-y-coed and Llanrwst, and this diminished the importance of the Chester to Holyhead route. By 1828, the new Telford road (now the A5) through Betws-y-coed and then across the Menai Suspension Bridge was faster by $3^1/_4$ hours than the old road from Chester. By 1828, out of 11 coaches from London to Holyhead, only one passed through Northop, so the fate of the Yacht was sealed. It continued as a coaching inn until 1874, when it closed its doors and became a private house – renamed Plymouth House.

22. A LONG WALK BACK TO LLANFOR
JOHN WILLIAMS' TOMBSTONE

Llanfor was originally called 'Llanfawr' (the 'Great Llan') and was one of the largest parishes in northern Wales. Its church dedicated to a Celtic Saint, St Deiniol, and an inscription in the church:

CAVO SENIARGII

CAVO LIES HERE, SON OF SENIAGII

is probably 6th Century and suggests an old foundation. It is mentioned for taxation purposes in 1254 and, with the motte and bailey castle near the church, Llanfor was an important place in the 13th Century. Prince Llywelyn ap Gruffudd summoned his brother, Dafydd, to 'Llanfawr in Penllyn' in 1274 for an examination of charges against him. It had a weekly market and an annual fair, but lost these to Bala, a mile away, when a royal charter granted Bala borough status in 1324. Llanfor continued as the centre of a large parish and this may explain a geography of burial in the

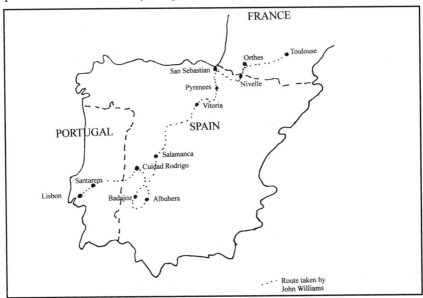

Peninsula War. John Williams' route and battles.

churchyard, with the different villages and hamlets allocated their own patch of consecrated ground. Rhosygwaliau, Cwm Tirmynach, Capel Celyn and other areas have their own section of the cemetery; the Quakers from Ciltalgarth have their own spot near the main path, which is now convenient for American tourists. Most of the gravestones are in slate and inscribed in Welsh, but there are notable exceptions where English surnames – Cooper, Dutton, Hinds – recall the incoming families who came to work on the Rhiwlas Estate. One of the strangest tombstones – in English, near the eastern corner of Tower – is to a local soldier who survived twenty-seven battles during the Napoleonic Wars. The neatly inscribed slate stone records the main battles in which John Williams fought and survived until his burial here at the age of eighty-seven. At the time he joined the army, Britain was at war with France, under Napoleon, which occupied most of continental Europe except Russia.

The first battle recorded on the headstone is Martinique – the main island base of the French in the West Indies. In 1809, the 23rd Foot Regiment of the Royal Welsh Fusiliers landed on the island after a naval blockade. The army stormed the fort and for its distinguished conduct in the campaign, the Regiment was permitted to bear the word 'Martinique' on its colours. Many losses were due to yellow fever and some islands were so pestilential that diseases such as yellow fever killed more men than warfare.

On his return from the West Indies, John Williams, an infantryman in the 23rd Foot Regiment, landed in Lisbon in Portugal in November 1810. This was the only part of the Iberian Peninsula then occupied by the British army under Wellington's command. The area east of Lisbon was protected by a line of hills and ditches known as the 'Lines of Torre Vedras', which was a defensive layout to protect Lisbon for supplies from Britain to get through to the port. The first major battle against the formidable French army was at Albuera on 16 May 1811, with heavy casualties on both sides. In the battle, the British infantry were drawn up in squares and, with muskets drawn, had to withstand the onslaught of the French lancers on horseback. Many soldiers died in their ranks as they stood and were replaced by soldiers standing behind

Tombstone of John Williams in Llanfor churchyard listing some of the 27 battles he fought in: Matinique, Albuhera, Cuidad, Rodrigo, Badajoz, Salamanca, Vitoria, Pyrenees, St Sebastian, Nivelle, Orthez, Toulouse, Waterloo.

them. A year later, the battlefield was still showing evidence of the carnage – it was covered in white bones, cartridge boxes, pieces of belts, torn clothing and blood-stained shoes. On each side, four thousand men were killed, but now Wellington was ready to push deeper into Spain.

There were two key frontier posts – Cuidad Rodrigo and Badajoz. The British army moved slowly over rough tracks and often in torrential rains, which blocked the heavy guns being moved on carts. After a siege, Cuidad Rodrigo was taken after cannon fire had breached the weak masonry of the wall and a final hand-to-hand bayonet charge. The next fort was Badajoz, which was a recently built castle on a hill-top summit with curtain walls, towers and a deep ditch below. The British soldiers charged up the slope during hours of darkness in April but encountered mines, booby-traps, grenades, cannon balls and lighted powder barrels which were rolled down the slope and brilliantly lit up the battle scene. The soldiers had to pass through a 'minefield' (chevaux de frise) of sharp sword blades set upright in the ground. Losses were heavy and heaps of bodies littered the slopes and filled the wet ditch but eventually, a column of infantry broke through the wall by scaling ladders, and Badajoz was taken.

In the hot summer of 1812, the long march on Salamanca started and here, another fierce battle – also recorded in Llanfor churchyard – took place. Conditions had improved for the army – adequate bread, beef and plenty of Spanish wine helped to improve morale. The next stage was through fertile valleys and mountains clothed in chestnut oaks as they approached Victoria, capital of a Basque province. Wellington was faced with a large French army of 60,000 men and 150 guns across the river Zadona.

Against them, Wellington pushed forward with 80,000 men with 70 guns in four immense columns. The battle raged from 10 a.m. until after 6 p.m. on the longest day of 1813, and the French army was forced to retreat towards passes through the Pyrenees. They left practically all their guns, immense quantities of ammunition, stores, carriages, military chests full of money, mules and horses. There were 5,000 casualties on both sides, but the British forced the French through the Pyrenees and they reached the coast at San Sebastian. San Sebastian was a difficult place to besiege – a rocky peninsula between a tidal river and the Bay of Biscay, with a surrounding wall and castle. A garrison of 3,000 seasoned French infantry and gunners kept the Allied armies out. Eventually, after the old medieval wall had been breached and the houses in the town were in ruins, an attack by infantry poured through the walls. The French were driven from house to house until the town was taken, but only after 3,700 allied casualties. The army then pressed on to the French frontier down the Nivelle valley, where another battle was fought. These were desperate times for the French after Napoleon had retreated from Russia. The British and Spanish army continued to advance deeper into France with the capture of Orthez and the final battle at Toulouse. Napoleon abdicated, and the Peninsula War was over.

After a short exile on the Island of Elba, Napoleon returned to France in March 1815, and Wellington had to reassemble his army in Belgium. The final battle was at Waterloo, where Wellington and the Prussians decisively defeated Napoleon but, again, with heavy losses on both sides.

To have survived twenty-seven battles, including the major ones in Spain, shows that John Williams had great physical and mental resources as well as courage. The battles of the Peninsula War were notoriously fiercely fought with cannon, mines, bayonets, lances, swords, muskets, grenades and incendiary bombs and lighted kegs of gunpowder. Apart from this, there were the privations of food shortage, fierce heat and harsh cold, as well as periodic torrential rain. He returned to Llanfor for the rest of his life – forty-one years – and is fittingly remembered by his regiment – the 23rd (Royal Welsh Fusiliers) Regiment of Foot.

23. THE GATE-POSTS HAVE BEEN MOVED
THE ARCHAEOLOGY OF TURNPIKE ROADS

'Turnpike' refers to a spiked barrier placed across a road, and it came into use after 1700, when Acts of Parliament gave local bodies, called 'Turnpike Trustees', powers to erect these barriers and levy tolls which could be used to improve roads. By 1752, the need for better roads in north-eastern Wales led to the setting up of Turnpike Trusts. To qualify as a trustee, a man had to have an annual income of £80 or real estate valued at £2,000. With other trustees, he would advertise in the local papers his intention to establish a Turnpike Trust and, if they agreed, they would get an Act of Parliament covering a section of road in their area. They then bought land, built toll-houses, erected gates or chains, and appointed surveyors and toll-keepers. They then leased the gates for auction and the toll-keepers used the income to improve the roads. The Trustees carried out an annual audit of costs and income. They disapproved of vehicles which damaged surfaces, especially heavy, narrow-wheeled vehicles. They exempted some

*Rhydymain Toll House
– 'Charges at this Gate'.*

vehicles from paying tolls – military, church and chapel-goers, funerals, carts carrying stone or lime for farms and horses being taken to the smithy for shoeing. The tolls were unpopular, and some methods of toll-evasion were used; hiding farm produce under stone was a frequent method. The annual audit gave the profit made and also showed the busiest roads. As late as 1869, the Broughton-Pontblyddyn road collected £590 in tolls. The tolls were usually shown on a board on the wall of the toll-house and in some places, they were inscribed on a slate board such as the one which survives at Rhyd-y-main toll house near Dolgellau.

121

Apart from toll-houses and gates, the Turnpike Trusts were expected to set up milestones to give the distances to the nearest towns; many of these have survived, though badly weathered and sometimes hidden in the hedge-rows. The penalty for defacing or damaging a milestone was forty shillings. The Broughton-Pontblyddyn Turnpike Trust existed from 1756 until 1882, and is shown on the 1880 O.S. map. There is an interesting survival of the old road system and its 'landscape' near one of the old toll-houses at Camfa Rhinallt. Apart from the toll-house, there is a milestone cut in the masonry of Rhyd-y-Defaid Bridge, another milestone near Pontblyddyn, a smithy and, until recently, the original toll-gate. This fine example of a wooden toll-gate had been removed from Camfa Rhinallt toll-house – a short distance away – to be used as a field gate. These toll-gates are well recorded in drawings by Frances Grey and have a distinctive Flintshire regional style. The Camfa Rhinallt gate and the others were held in place by two pillars of white limestone. The limestone was composed of fossil-rich rock with crinoid and brachiapod shells and calcite veins.

Old Turnpike Trust Milestone near Pontblyddyn (c.1756) still legible – Chester – 9 miles now set back from road.

Outcrop rocks like these are found near Maeshafn, two miles west of Mold. The pillars are five and a half feet high, have a diameter of one foot and have a distinctive rounded top. The main pillar holding the gate has a pole through the centre, drilled to the base. From this iron pole, a long horizontal bar ran along the length of the top of the gate. At the bottom, there was an iron hinge and pier to enable the gate to revolve and open. On the opposite pillar, there was a bar-slot for opening and closing; this pillar was near or alongside the toll-house. Five horizontal wooden bars and four uprights completed the 'Flintshire' gate and made a sturdy eight-foot wide barrier. The original gate at Camfa Rhinallt had miraculously survived

Turnpike Trust Gate (replica) with original gateposts at Y Fferm, Pontblyddyn.

almost undamaged as a nearby field-gate until it was recently removed. The limestone gate-posts were removed and a replica gate set up on the drive to the Elizabethan manor-house of Y Fferm at Pontblyddyn, about one mile from the original site. The old gate was not considered worth re-hanging and an exact replica was hung between the two limestone posts and gives an uncanny reminder of the Turnpike Era. The gates and posts were designed to a local specification and pillars, which have survived at Buckley, Llandegla and other places, can be readily identified.

There is no complete list of the toll-houses in Flintshire, but Frances Gray's drawings, made in 1880, show eleven gates and toll-houses which were still operating and often with the toll-keeper standing outside the two-roomed cottage. A large number of these cottages still exist, some have been modernized and reach prices of £100,000. Some of the lonely moorland cottages, however, are still in their original condition. A good example is 'Tyrpeg Cottage' on the moorland road above Pentrefoelas. Built in 1826 when the Denbigh-Pentrefoelas Turnpike (now the A543) was completed, it has survived intact and has impressive sweeping views of the road. The toll-keepers would have been on constant alert, particularly on the Post Roads, for the approach of the Mail

Coach. They would be ready for the coach to pass through without interruption. Failure to open the gates for the Mail Coach to pass through at speed – about 10 miles per hour – would lead to heavy fines. To be easily identified, the toll-keeper wore a tall black hat, corduroy breeches, white stockings and – for collecting tolls – a bag or white apron. They had to be on their best behaviour and were expected to tolerate people who resented paying tolls. Despite their efforts and the improved road conditions, the toll-gates and keepers were unpopular. In the mid-18th Century, riots erupted – the Rebecca Riots were the best known – in which gates were battered down and toll-houses burnt to the ground. The Turnpike system lasted until the 1880's and were finally abolished in Flintshire in 1889 and replaced by the Highways Board whereby roads became the responsibility of the local Councils and were financed by rates.

Apart from the toll-houses and milestones, which still recall the days of the Turnpike Trusts, most of the roads have become our modern roads. However, in some places, the old Turnpike Roads have been preserved, notably between Pentrefoelas and Capel Curig where Telford – from 1815 onwards – constructed his London-Holyhead Road and, in sections, did not use the old Turnpike. His main aim was to reduce the gradient of the new road, so parts of the Turnpike in the Conwy gorge north of Pentrefoelas were too steep. No horse was reduced to walking pace from London to Holyhead so that the Holyhead Mail had an average speed of $10^1/2$ miles per hour for its entire journey, including stops. Many of these old Turnpike sections are minor roads, farm tracks and 'green roads', which have become overgrown. James Barfoot made an interesting study of an old Turnpike road from Machynlleth to Aberystwyth. He excavated sections of the road and found four main periods of building from 1769 – the first Act of Parliament granting a Turnpike Trust for this road – until 1834, when the road was by-passed by a road nearer the coast where the gradient was easier. In the bottom layers of the road, he found slabs and pebbles and evidence of use by coaches from the finds of horse-shoe nails, a split-pin and a square-headed tyre nail. In the next layer, he found a mixture of sandy clay, gravel,

Turnpike Cottage (with nameplate) on the A543 (Denbigh-Pentrefoelas) in its original condition, 1826. Still occupied.

Turnpike Trust Toll House near Padeswood.

Machynlleth-Aberystwyth Turnpike Road under the surface of the road exposed showing coach-wheel ruts in this steep section (right-hand side). Considerable braking would be necessary on descending.

pebbles and rubble and, unexpectedly, several pieces of Buckley pottery – a thick red to pink ware with black manganese glaze. Buckley was then the most famous pottery-making centre in northern Wales. There was a demand for troughs and mugs for storing water and milk. Most farms in the Machynlleth area had a dairy where water would be piped into a large trough, which would act as a reservoir for cooling the milk, which would then be stored in large Buckley mugs before the days of refrigeration. It is not surprising that large quantities of discarded Buckley pottery was used in resurfacing the local Turnpike roads. In the upper sections excavated, the road builders (1820-34) used the new methods employed by the famous road engineer, John McAdam. The new surface was made of small broken stones and clay rammed into a cambered surface of extreme hardness. This surface was laid between drystone kerbs and this was the final surface before the Turnpike Trust road near Machynlleth was by-passed in 1834. In one steep section near Derwen-las, the grass-covered road was excavated to reveal exposed rock, which had been hand-chiselled in a clearly-marked herringbone pattern with a deep drainage gutter, also chiselled, in the rock, along the sides of the road. This steep rock section must have been a problem for coaches, and there is clear evidence of wheel-ruts made by the coaches, which were four foot eight and a half inches apart. This was the width of the coach, and the ruts indicated that the brakes had been applied on this section. In this way, archaeology can give a record of the construction phases and materials used by the Turnpike Trusts and give an insight into coach travel.

24. THE PONTFADOG OAK

The common oak (Quercus robur) flourishes in the Ceiriog valley, where dense forests still cover the hill-slopes. In the Middle Ages, this forest was more complete and almost impenetrable and forced Henry II in his 'invasion' of 1165 to send a large body of wood-cutters ahead of his mercenary army. Much of this forest still survives and is shown by the abundance of place-names such as 'llwyn' (grove), 'coed' (wood), 'fedw' (birch), 'celyn' (holly), and 'gwern' (alder). It is claimed that near the village of Pontfadog, there is the oldest oak tree in Britain, which is still growing. Measuring its girth at 5 feet from the ground surface, it is 42 feet, which is considered to be the record and an index of its age. It is still healthy and growing each year with an annual crop of leaves, but the interior of the tree has been partly hollowed-out due to ageing. A photograph taken 110 years ago is on display in the local pub, the Swan Inn, and shows hardly any change to the surviving lower half of the tree. Calculations based on its width suggest that it could have been growing since early medieval times, but no exact date has been accepted. It has even enveloped stone walls and gateposts and a local farmer, aged 93, claimed that in his lifetime he had seen it grow. The growth of the outer layers is still healthy with new wood growing and supporting a dense canopy of branches and leaves, which gives good shade in summer. There maybe special reasons for the growth of a tree beyond its 'allotted span' due to adverse soil and climate, which may have caused initial slow growth. Its ability to lose its dead upper boughs is also thought to slow the ageing process and its isolated position – similar to the great oaks found in parklands – is another factor favouring old age. It has good genes and its acorns have been collected for botanical research and propagation.

The age of a tree can only be precisely determined when it is cut down and the annual, mainly summer, rings are counted. This method of tree-dating is known as dendrochronology. The same method of calculation can be used for dating timbers used in old houses and churches, provided the timber has retained the radial section of the tree. By measuring the width of each annual ring, an

Pontfadog oak.

unique sequence – similar to a bar-code on a supermarket product – can record the life history of a tree and the date when it was cut and used for building. By using the 'bar-code' of a recently-chopped tree, a radial section of a beam in a house and the rings of ancient trees left in submerged coastal forests or peat beds, a chronology, or time-scale, can be made. Thicker annual rings would indicate warmer and wetter summers and so clues to past climate as for a prehistoric time can be gained. For oak trees along the Welsh Border, AD 1055 – just before the Norman invasion of England – was hot and wet! The archaeological value of tree-ring dating or dendro-chronology ('dendro'-tree) is a valuable guide to the date of a building. Fortunately, many medieval carpenters used planks cut radially, so that only the bark and sapwood have been lost, but, in some cases, even unpeeled bark has been used for beams, especially in servants' quarters in the attics. A timber building known to have been built in the 13th Century in Much Wenlock used timber beams from an oak tree which started growing in AD 886. Part of the beam is now on display at Ludlow Museum and the section showing the annual rings has been neatly polished to show the individual years and the climatic fluctuations over this long period.

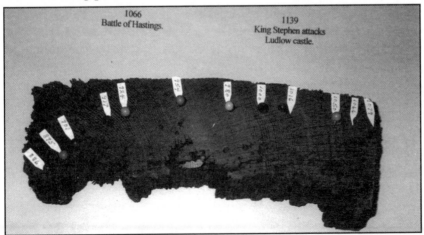

Oak beam from 13th Century house at Much Wenlock from oak tree traceable to its origin in AD 886 in Ludlow Museum.
(Copyright: Shropshire County Council)

25. SHEEP ON THE TRACKS
THE INDUSTRIAL ARCHAEOLOGY OF A
'GHOST VILLAGE' – ARENNIG

Arennig is now a 'ghost village' with practically no recorded history. Its story is almost entirely dependent on memories and oral history. A few houses survive – five at the moment – from its hey-day in the 1930's, when it was a thriving community with up to 40 schoolchildren. It was the product of a quarry cut into the northern flanks of Arennig Fawr, from which it got its name. There is no evidence of a settlement here before 1882, when the Bala-Ffestiniog railway was built along the sides of the Tryweryn valley from Bala to its highest point – Prysor Halt – on the shores of Llyn Tryweryn. From here, the railway descended rapidly into the Prysor valley over a spectacular viaduct and a narrow ledge cut into the steep hillside. The building of the Prysor viaduct was a major engineering feat and brought hundreds of navvies, who were housed in farmhouses and barns, as well as special railway 'carriages'. The riverside pub at Rhyd Fen was extended to provide a dormitory and the barn at Bwlch y Buarth was used. Two houses were built for railway workers to supervise and maintain the railway in this bleak area with heavy winter rain and snow. By 1901, a large house at Plas Bodrenig is shown on the O.S. map and a converted granary above the stable (llofft ystabl) became the first chapel. The Puleston-Jones family lived at Plas Bodrenig with its six bedrooms, a cellar and garden and a private path to the railway station. A surveyor from Bala – Evan Jones – had married into a wealthy Denbighshire family called the Pulestons and, as Puleston-Jones, he built Plas Bodrenig with the intention of extracting a hard coarse rock – a type of granite called quartz-latite – suitable for road surfaces and as ballast, forming the track-bed of railways. Houses were built for quarrymen, including a row of six terraced cottages – Voelas View – which had partly survived until the 1980's, but now only survives as a foundation level. The village grew along the road as a ribbon development. Another chapel was built – a 'zinc' chapel, which held some social events such as eisteddfodau and whist drives. Another building, which was not

*Bala to Blaenau Ffestiniog Railway Track
– now disused near Arennig.*

directly connected with the quarry, was Bodrenig Farm, which provided local meat and milk from its sheep and cattle. The flat valley floor was mainly coarse grass, which was liable to flooding, and its main use was for peat digging. Most of the houses and the station have been demolished, but the railway track, with its embankment cuttings and drainage culvert bridges, has survived and, in places, has become a footpath and grazing land for sheep. Two buildings which have survived are the 'zinc' chapel and the magazine, which was vital to the running of the quarry. It was a small, solidly built stone hut, which was tarred regularly to keep the powder dry. Access through a small arched door was restricted to two 'creigwyr' who collected the powder every day. It was situated on an isolated bank outside the village, and was strictly out-of-bounds. Apart from the two vertical faces of the quarry, the only surviving evidence of quarrying are the two concrete pillars across the road, which supported the bridge which carried the track to the crusher. This large area of railway station, sidings and the crusher is now a flat area, which is used for car parking for visitors. The crusher produced the fine granite chippings, which can be seen along the former railway track. A narrow-gauge railway ran from the station to a small quarry called 'Y Foty', where cubic setts of hard dolerite were made on site and then transported in one-ton trucks to Arennig station, about a mile away. The quarry produced setts for road surfaces in many towns in northern Wales and Lancashire at the beginning of the 20th Century. The narrow rail track can still be clearly seen as a ledge along the hillside with culverts, embankments and, especially, the ruts of the rail track often water-filled! This sett quarry at 'Y Foty' was abandoned about 1910, and the quarrymen transferred to the main quarry at Arennig.

The main quarry at Arennig was opened up about 1906-8, although a very small local quarry had existed earlier and was used for building stone locally. The new quarry was opened up by Puleston-Jones on the vertical crags of Clogwyn y Frân, which projected as a sill from the base of Arennig Fawr. The quarry was worked at two levels and each quarryman worked on the higher or lower bank. This was the usual method of working in the great slate quarries of northern Wales using a system of galleries (ponciau). The Arennig Granite Company drew workmen from Bala, who came up on the 6.30 am train from Bala and returned on the 5 pm train at the end of the shift. Other workers came from the nearest villages – Rhyd Uchaf, Capel Celyn and Llidiardau, as well as Arennig village. About forty men worked in the quarry in the 1920's and 1930's. The rockman was responsible for drilling holes and then filling them with powder brought in daily from the magazine, and then lighting the fuse to set the blast. Each man worked in a section of the gallery and its profitability depended on the rock formation, particularly the joint surfaces of the rock, and how much rock fell at each blast. The men then had to break the resulting mass of debris with sledgehammers, then fill the wagons and move them to the weighing machines. Two or three wagons at a time would then be released along the overhead rail track, over the bridge, to the huge crusher on the railway. The stone was crushed into various sizes, with coarse chippings being used for road surfaces and rail track foundations. The breaking of the stone by hand was the toughest job and the men were on piece-work; the more wagons they could fill the more wages they got and there was always a 'race' to the weighing machines, where the load was tallied and payments calculated.

Arennig. The remains of the magazine where powder
for blasting at the quarry was stored.

In this hard environment, accidents occurred from time to time; causes would include blasting, breaking up the hard rock, climbing the steep gallery walls, rock falls as well as the dangers from heavy rain and snowfall. One accident, which occurred in 1910, involved a rockman, who had to scale the vertical quarry face each day. At the top of the face, he wedged an iron spike into the flat surface, attached a rope to the spike and then around his waist and abseiled down the face to a predetermined spot, where he drilled a hole into which he placed powder and lit the fuse. The slow-burning fuse allowed him to ascend the face to the top of the gallery before the blast discharged the fresh debris on to the floor below. On the day of the accident, he was asked to try out a faster fuse and this time, he failed to get back to the top and was thrown on to the slope and deeply gashed his leg. Blood poured out of the wound and he risked permanent injury. Fortunately, a down-valley train had arrived at the station and the driver, who was trained in first aid, staunched the blood flow and the rockman was taken to the hospital at Bala. He was partially disabled, but managed to get another job at the quarry checking the wagon loads. A number of men retired early due to quarry dust and a feature of life in Arennig was the daily covering of fine dust, which hung over the village and coated the workers.

Arennig's dependence on the railway was fully revealed in 1960, when Liverpool completed the dam below Capel Celyn village, which became the huge Celyn reservoir for Liverpool's water supply. Parts of the new lake drowned the railway track, and the cost of a replacement of track at a higher level was considered uneconomic. For a while, the quarrymen came in by bus, but the costs of the transport of granite by road reduced its competitiveness; production declined and the village was abandoned.

The most 'atmospheric' route to Arennig is the road from Bala via Rhyd Uchaf and Llidiardau and then following the edge of a huge peat-bog – Ffridd y Fawnog – at the eastern foot of Arennig Fawr. This peat-bog is literally a quagmire even in the driest spell as its local name – Siglen (quaking ground) – indicates and is best avoided on foot. Getting a foundation for its one electricity pylon was an engineering feat. Before reaching Arennig, the old railway line can be seen on the right-hand side and then the road enters the old village at a cluster of houses, including Bwlch y Buarth. The road continues through the 'village' passing 'Isallt', with a footpath on the right to the once-forbidden magazine, the zinc chapel and the final house, Coedlle. The quarry lies to the left after passing the bridge pillars, which once led to the crusher, and at the car park the full extent of the quarry can be seen.

26. THE FORD OF THE GRAVES
LLYN ALED ISAF RESERVOIR

In 1914, in the remotest part of the wild moorland of Mynydd Hiraethog (Denbigh Moors), a footbridge over the river Aled at Rhyd-y-Bedd ('the crossing of the grave') marked the point where a moorland road crossed the river, but was the limit for cars. The area around was rough grass and heather, with one small sheep farm – Waen-isaf-las – some sheepfolds and, near the highest point (1,500 feet), a shepherd's hut in the midst of summer sheep pasture. Below the footbridge, the river Aled plunged over a steep waterfall

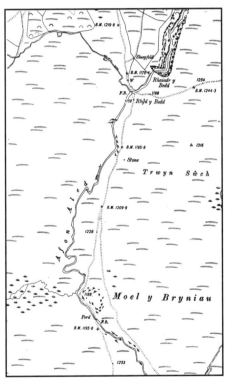

– Rhaeadr-y-Bedd ('waterfall of the grave') into a narrow rock-walled gorge. The moors, above the footbridge, with its marsh and water-retaining peat beds, were a perfect collecting ground for the heavy rainfall. Being unpopulated and unpolluted, it was suitable for a big reservoir to satisfy the demand for water from the coastal resort of Rhyl, where demand soared during the summer.

In 1931, the spot just above the waterfall was chosen as the site of the large dam to impound the reservoir and land acquired along the Aled valley and the natural lake – Llyn Aled. The natural bank holding back Llyn Aled since its formation after the Ice Age, was raised, and this gave extra storage water to

Llyn Aled Isaf Reservoir.
The dam built at Rhyd-y-Bedd. The reservoir
drowned the Afon Aled as far as the sheepfold.
The valley as it was in 1880.

Llyn Aled Isaf – the Dam at Rhyd-y-Bedd.

feed into the new lower reservoir – Llyn Aled Isaf.

Work started in 1934, and was a major engineering project in an area with access problems and no labour available locally. Fortunately, there was plenty of rock available, and labour could be drawn in from a wide area. Practically no heavy machinery was used and, apart from cement, the builders used hard manual labour and local resources. The site of the dam was the head of the rock-bound gorge above the waterfall, where it was narrow and had a good foundation of solid rock. Machines were set up on the site for grinding and cutting the stone and a machine for winching the stone up from the quarry below the site of the dam. A storage shed for keeping the cement – brought in bags by lorry – was built. The rock was ground to gravel and crushed to powder and then fed into a concrete mixer. The mixture was then poured into moulds to make large pre-cast blocks of concrete. The blocks were made by hand-labour and placed on wagons on a 'railway' pulled by hand to the site of the dam. Before the blocks were put in place, and then mortared and grouted, the builders had to drill a tunnel

A concrete block which was not used.

to carry the river to by-pass the dam. Hot pitch (tar) was also put into the concrete to keep it 'warm', and this process would seal any cracks which might subsequently develop in the face of the dam. A winch lifted the blocks from the wagons and was also used to lower the pre-cast blocks to the builders.

The labour-force came in daily from the area around – walking mainly over a distance of 5 to 10 miles, though some came across the moorland road on motor bikes. They came from as far as Bylchau, Pentrefoelas and Cerrigydrudion, the farthest point. In an area of sparsely-populated hill farms, the organizing of a labour force of about eighty men at the peak of building (1935-7) was difficult. Many of the jobs involved specialised work such as blasting, quarrying, masonry work, surveying and carpentry. Some of the workers stayed during the week at the two nearest farms – Glan y Gors and Nant y Merddyn. In Glan y Gors – the nearest farm to the site only two-thirds of a mile away – the farmer built a shed with a brick fireplace and chimney for cooking and heating. They stayed here for six days a week and returned home for

Sundays. The weather here, at over 1,200 feet above the sea level, was severe in winter – heavy rain, low temperatures and thick snow cover. The only archaeological remains of their lodgings at Glan y Gors is the ruined brick 'talcen', which is the gable end of the hut shown by the fireplace and chimney.

Little reliance was placed on machinery except the cement mixers, which used cement brought in regularly by lorry and stored in sacks in the site. A diesel machine for crushing the rock was also important. Very few amenities were provided – an office at the hub of administration, a canteen for meals and a shop mainly selling tobacco and cigarettes.

For its time, the dam was large and the impounded reservoir stretched back for a mile above the old footbridge at Rhyd-y-Bedd, along the bottom of the valley. The area which was drowned was mainly rough grass and marsh, used only for sheep grazing. The road was resurfaced and, in places, raised above the old road and continued across the dam to Llansannan. The reservoir drains a large catchment area of heavy rainfall, marshy land, water-retaining peat and two natural lakes – Llyn Aled and Llyn y Foel Frech.

Looking down from the dam, there is enough industrial archaeology to reconstruct the working conditions here from 1935 to 1939. The most evident sign is the huge quarry cut into the left bank of the river. The stone was raised to a flat terrace above, with concrete remains of buildings involved in lifting the rock and crushing it. A perfectly-level concrete floor is all that remains of the cement-storage shed. The tramway for the wagons bringing the moulded concrete blocks to the masons working on the dam is clearly visible. Some of these blocks have been left behind on the surface and, in their unweathered state, are witness to the quality of the work sixty-five years ago. The project was completed in June 1939, when the long, underground pipeline to Rhyl was completed. It was just in time – three months later the Second World War started.

27. TREASURE HUNT FOR RED SANDSTONE
VALE OF CLWYD

It is possible to cross the length and breadth of the Vale of Clwyd without seeing any solid rocks, except on the edges of the Vale. The landscape is of river meadows, grassy hills, belts of trees and neat hedgerows. The solid geology appears to be a mystery and yet the area has been mapped and details of the underground rocks are known. Boreholes and wells have penetrated to the water-bearing rocks and prove that the red sandstone is 530 metres thick under Ruthin – 'the Red Fortress'. The area was part of a vast Tropical Desert in Triassic times and was part of a continuous inland plain with Cheshire, Lancashire and its 'twin' – the Eden valley in Cumbria. Wind-blown sand-dunes were scattered across this desert basin and later became compacted to form massive beds of red sandstone. To the casual observer, these beds are visible in road and rail cuttings, patches of red soil, a few disused quarries and, in Ruthin, the grounds of the castle.

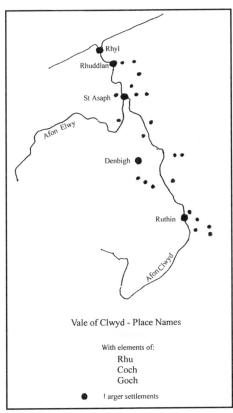

Vale of Clwyd - Place Names

With elements of:
Rhu
Coch
Goch

● ! arger settlements

Usually, the best clues to the rocks of an area are the building stones of the churches, castles and old houses which date back to a time when bricks were not used and the transport of stone on unmaintained roads and tracks was difficult and expensive. The medieval masons, who built the churches, sought out the nearest rock, which was

Ruthin castle. Entrances to underground passages and dungeons.

usually in the parish itself – the 'parish rock'. In Northop, the local
sandstone was found in the parish, about a mile from the church –
down Quarry Lane – and in northern Wales, rock was usually
available locally. But in the Vale of Clwyd, there were problems –
there was limestone in the hills on the edge of the Vale but the main
rock, which was red sandstone, only outcropped in a few places.
The best clues to these outcrops were the occurrence of place-
names (usually in Welsh) which showed good local knowledge of
the geology. The medieval builders decided to use limestone for
the main building and used the red sandstone for ornamental work
in windows, doorways and, inside, pillars, columns and arches.
Out of the twenty-eight churches in the Vale of Clwyd, only four
were built entirely of sandstone.

A useful indicator of red sandstone outcrops is the old Welsh
word 'Rhudd', which occurs commonly in the Vale. The word itself
has died out in oral and living Welsh, but still survives in
compound adjectives or descriptive words such as 'Rhudd-goch'
(rosy-cheeked, blush), 'Rhudd-em' (ruby) and 'Rhudd-aur' (red
gold). There are many place-names in the vale where 'Rhudd', or

abbreviations of it, occur and in each place it is associated with the location of a red sandstone outcrop and is a certain guide to the local geology as in:

Rhuthun
Llanrhudd
Rhuallt
Rhuddlan
Bodrhyddan

Another certain indicator of red sandstone is the Welsh name for 'red' as in 'coch' or 'goch' and use in the name of a house as in:

Tŷ Coch (Red house)
Plas Coch (Red mansion)
Cefn Coch (Red ridge)
Pentre Coch (Red village)

These names are repeated on the Ordnance Survey maps and show how, in the past, people have identified the sandstone and used it

Plas Coch (Ruthin). Built originally in 13th Century. Rebuilt of sandstone blocks in 1613.

Llanbedr Old Church. Main west doorway and part of Belfry Tower – in New Red Sandstone.

to build their houses, farms and even mansions. There are also some isolated spots where the sandstone is found in stream beds, river banks and disused quarries. In the hamlet of Hirwaen, when digging a deep pit for a septic tank, the owner was surprised that, when digging through a thick layer of reddish soil, he hit hard layers of red sandstone. Just outside the hamlet, the road passes through a deep cutting with massive sandstone beds exposed on both sides. Hirwaen itself, with its own 'Tŷ-coch', owes its existence to this patch of hard sandstone and further up the valley the river has cut through thick beds which, in the 19th Century and earlier, were extensively quarried for building stone. These quarries leave little documentary record – there are no bills, invoices or production figures – and a visit to the Record Office yields only an old O.S. map (1874), which shows the extent of the quarry faces at that time. They are now overgrown by bushes and oak trees, forgotten even by the local inhabitants.

The quarry stands on the north side of the valley below Fron Ganol. It is a 50 foot vertical cliff devoid of vegetation or debris and is still as freshly exposed as the time it was abandoned. The red sandstone consists of massive beds of hard rock, which would have been much sought after as a building stone from the Middle Ages to the 19th Century. The 1874 First Edition O.S. map shows it as a 'disused quarry'. Above the quarry face, the road from Fron Ganol would have been used by horse and cart to transport the stone to areas around Ruthin. No records exist to give production figures and where the stone was sold. When it was abandoned, the face was left as a continuous straight wall, suggesting a clear-cut final decision to close. Although no documents exist, there is some archaeological evidence. There are two iron spikes drilled into the wall at about the same level and footholds have been left. The most valuable evidence is a fine inscription:

ERW
1850

cut by a stonemason, and which must record its final working date. The fine quality of the stone is shown by the absence of weathering from frost or water in the subsequent 163 years.

The only four churches built of red sandstone (15th Century) – Llangynhafal, Llandyrnog, Llangwyfan and Llanbedr (now ruined) – are the only all-sandstone churches in the Vale. The first three are, however, cement rendered to protect the sandstone from weathering. The old hill-top church at Llanbedr, although now badly ruined, provides good evidence of the use of red sandstone in medieval times. There are three arched doorways, the remains of a bell-cote tower and it has large sandstone blocks used as door jambs. The iron hinges of the main west door are intact and the long bar-slots for closing the door are carved in the sandstone. The churchyard is almost completely overgrown in this 'lost church', but some gravestones are still readable and date from 1740's to 1850, when the church was closed and replaced by the limestone church on the Ruthin-Mold road at Llanbedr.

In other churches around Ruthin, the primary building material is limestone, but red sandstone is used randomly in the walls and especially in the doorways and windows, where it was easier to work into tracery and mullions. Inside the church at Llanfwrog, there is a double nave separated by an arcade with three piers or shafts dividing pointed arches, all made of smooth red sandstone. In the visitors' book there is a rare geological comment – 'it is a stunning sandstone church' – which shows an appreciation of

Llanfwrog church. Four sandstone shafts support three fine pointed arches which separate the double nave.

these fine arches. A short distance from the church, on the Bont Uchel Road, there is a disused quarry dating back to 1815, when the new Turnpike Trust road to Cerrigydrudion from Ruthin was being built. The quarry lies on a small outcrop of red sandstone and a nearby wall points out its location.

The best evidence of this use of red sandstone inside the church is seen in St Peter's church in Ruthin, where the double nave is also divided by a colonnade of five sandstone pillars surmounted by five pointed arches, which support the spectacular 16th Century oak roof. The roof is the finest example of medieval timber-work in Wales. The church was built in 1310 by John de Grey as a collegiate church, with cloisters where the college of priests lived. Parts of the walls of these cloisters and the adjoining church tower are built of red sandstone, although the tower was extended to its full height in limestone. A short distance to the south, across the market square, lies Ruthin castle, originally known as 'Castell Coch' (the Red Castle). Built in the latter part of the 13th Century, the castle was given by Edward I to Reginald de Grey, who became Lord of Dyffryn Clwyd. Substantial remains of the castle survive, with two corner towers of red sandstone, a moat cut in sandstone, mural passages in the curtain walls and basement chambers under the towers. The dungeons also survive with some of the underground passages through which defenders could run when the castle was under siege or being attacked. The castle was still, in 1586, according to Camden, 'a large and fair castle, which was used to entertain' and at that time had high towers and large, thick walls. But by 1632, it was in ruins and the stonework 'was not worth taking down and carrying away; it is easier to use the quarry which provided the stone for the castle'. Ruthin was not a walled town and this may account for the stories that underground sandstone tunnels from the castle led to vaults under some of the houses and inns in the town itself.

Most of the houses in Ruthin were built of limestone, or were half-timbered but one interesting, sandstone house, fittingly named 'Plas Coch', has survived. It was originally built in the 13th Century, but was entirely rebuilt of sandstone blocks from the castle quarry in 1613.

POSTSCRIPT

Having finished the book I planned a last visit to photograph the Turnpike Trust Toll-house – with its 'eyes on the road' – at Rhyd-y-Main. By chance two people visiting the cottage which was on sale had the key and permission to view. Noting my interest in local history they offered to show me around; unlike a stately home or castle a visit to a toll-house needs luck and some ingenuity! From the living-room there was a clear view of the Bala-Dolgellau road which would have given the toll-keeper ample time to see the horses, cattle, sheep, carriages and wagons before they reached the toll-gate across the road. The cottage built of local rock with a massive chimney and wide fireplace giving light, warmth and cooking for the toll-keeper's family. The bread-oven – a deep slot in the side of the fireplace – was still intact. An open stair-case led to the three small bedrooms with narrow windows set in the thick walls. The cottage was built after 1777 when the Bala-Dolgellau Turnpike Trust was set up and the present cottage was definitely recorded in 1828. A small garden at the back gave some privacy but the cottage was edge-on to the road where there was an abutment for the toll-gate.

Rhyd-y-Main Toll-house.

It was at this time (1797) that John Evans produced his famous map of northern Wales on a scale of three miles to one inch which was of great practical use for travellers. The map was noted for its accuracy showing roads, bridges and distances at every two miles on the main roads. Before 1790 there was no road from Bethesda to Capel Curig in the heart of Snowdonia. There were paths up the Nant Ffrancon valley to Llyn Ogwen but Thomas Pennant described it as 'the most dreadful horse-path in Wales worked in the rudest manner in steps for a great length'. Another track from Beddgelert to Capel Curig was so dangerous that a traveller in 1797 abandoned the path and – using John Evans' map – and took a diversion across the peat-covered base of Moel Siabod and was greatly relieved when he saw Dolwyddelan Castle in the distance. This situation was dramatically changed in 1791-2 when Lord Penrhyn, who was opening the slate quarries at Bethesda, made a road up the western side of Nant Ffrancon and continued it on to Capel Curig. This road – now a 'green road' – is used as a footpath today. The ruts made by the coach wheels are still imprinted on the

Lord Penrhyn's Road – coach-wheel ruts on old road (1790's) before the Turnpike Trusts.

rough stone surface of the old road. This road was shown on John Evans' map as a double line to show that it could be used by wheeled carriages. It was used by visitors to Lord Penrhyn's new inn – 'The Royal' – at Capel Curig. In 1792 when it was completed the road was described, perhaps optimistically, as 'firm and good; sufficiently commodions for carriages'.

To visit the toll-house at Rhyd-y-Main and to walk along the footpath from Capel Curig to Ogwen Cottage is to enjoy a vivid recollection of travel and the historical landscape in 1800.

London - Holyhead Mail-coach – built in 1826 at Bristol.
One of only two genuine mail-coaches existing today. Can be seen at Red House Working Carriage Museum, Darley Dale, Matlock, Derbyshire.

ACKNOWLEDGEMENTS

To the following people who helped to make writing this book a pleasure:

Dewi Parry Jones – who introduced me to the history of the Ceiriog valley.
Mike Hill – always able to find important documents at Flintshire Library H.Q.
Nick Todd – gave a professional finish to my maps.
Myrddin ap Dafydd – gave invaluable advice and encouragement.
John Lewis Jones – for remembering Arennig.
The owners/householders at Dolwen, Hafod Adam,
Cilgychwyn, Sarfle, Chweleriog Goch, Castell, Plymouth House and
     Caer Gai where I was given a warm welcome.
Canon John Evans who gave me access to Caerwys church.
Edward Besly
Rev. Sandra Roberts for access to Llandderfel Church.

The following organizations provided advice and information:

Grosvenor Museum, Chester
National Museum of Wales, Cardiff
British Museum, London
Gwynedd Archaeological Trust, Bangor
Bangor Museum
Clwyd-Powys Archaeological Trust, Welshpool
Record Offices at Caernarfon, Conwy, Dolgellau and Ruthin
Flintshire County Library
Ludlow Museum
Red House Carriage Museum